What Your Colleagues Are Saying . . .

"Constantly bombarded by new innovations that fail to yield promised results, education leaders often grow frustrated and discouraged. Rather than becoming skeptical of all innovations, DeWitt advises leaders to become thoughtfully discerning through the process of de-implementation. It's wise advice that is long overdue and vitally important."

—Thomas R. Guskey
Professor Emeritus, University of Kentucky
Lexington, KY

"STOP. We add, reform, innovate, and tinker but rarely consider how to reduce and halt that which has the least impact and distracts from the joy of teaching. DeWitt invites you to reflect, respond, and remove, and introduces the notion of efficiency into your life. This book in education is so overdue. It is the Konmari decluttering bible for schools."

—John Hattie
Emeritus Laureate Professor, University of Melbourne
Co-director of the Hattie Family Foundation
Carlton, Vic, Australia

"Schools are busy places that are often filled with the debris of failed initiatives. DeWitt's latest book tackles this unspoken challenge head-on. Highlighting the science of de-implementation and presenting a practical framework, his book is a must for any leader seeking support in clearing the decks in their buildings and empowering their teachers to focus on the important work of teaching."

—Tim O'Leary
Research Director, EDT
Lecturer, Melbourne Graduate School of Education
Parksville, Vic, Australia

"De-implementation is a core competency for any organization that focuses like a laser on only those high value initiatives that have real impact. DeWitt shows 'the why' behind implementation, and helps you map your own process and success criteria. If your leadership goal is to be more purposeful in where you focus your time, resources, and talent, *De-implementation* can help."

—Colleen Kaney
Assistant Superintendent, Hamburg Central School District
Hamburg, NY

"In *De-implementation: Creating the Space to Focus on What Works,* Peter M. DeWitt convincingly makes the case for getting serious about stopping or reducing (some) existing practices, and he provides no-nonsense tools to help you get this work done. It will help you to take the 'less-path', whilst also getting more done in the process!"

—Arran Hamilton
Group Education Director, Cognition Education, New Zealand
Author of *The Lean Education Manifesto* (Routledge) and
Building to Impact (Corwin)

"The pace and breadth of initiatives in schools seem to grow exponentially. *De-implementation* offers a much-needed sense of relief to step back and 'creates space to focus on what works.' The text reads like a conversation, offers a roadmap back to balance, and outlines a clear process and hands-on tools to support along the way."

—Chris Beals
Director, Washington Association of School Administrators
Instructional Leadership Network
Retired teacher, Building a District School Leader
Tumwater, WA

"My goal this year as a principal was to evaluate what we are doing in our building that is effective. As always, Peter M. DeWitt breaks down big ideas into immediate action steps that are simple. This book is timely for leaders in education because it is an opportunity to make evidence-based changes that focus on student learners and effective practices."

—Stacy Storey
Elementary Principal
Oklahoma City School District
Oklahoma City, OK

"After decades of adding on in public education, DeWitt's *De-implementation* guides readers through a thoughtful experience of reflection, wonder and questioning. He challenges decades of assumptions that more is better. Instead, he encourages more implementation of deep, important practices. Frankly, I will use the concept of 'clutter checks' for the rest of my career!

Like DeWitt says, 'It's now your turn!'"

—Michael Nelson
Retired Teacher, Building Leader Superintendent
2019 Washington state Superintendent of the Year
Assistant Executive Director at WASA
Enumclaw, WA

"A timely and necessary read, DeWitt challenges us teachers and leaders to look introspectively and consider what might we no longer need in education. The process of implementation should first look at what isn't serving our best interests and DeWitt provides a practical model to do so. All stakeholders who are responsible for initiatives and professional learning should read this book immediately. "

—Vince Bustamante
Author of *Great Teaching by Design* and *The Assessment Playbook for Distance and Blended Learning*
Edmonton AB, Canada

"Peter M. DeWitt has touched on a topic that so many school leaders have at times completely missed. *De-implementation* comes at a time when schools are being asked to take more on without considering what needs to be left behind. DeWitt's notion of de-implementation provides a platform for school communities to examine not just what they do but how and why they do it."

—Raymond Boyd
Principal, West Swan (Dayton) Primary School
West Swan, WA, Australia

"Due to the increased stress and complex issues currently compounding educational systems, there is no better time than now to read DeWitt's *De-implementation*. Filled with practical guidance, this book provides direction for educators to help navigate the de-implementation process. Specific steps are given for leaders and teachers to take together as they engage in critical conversations to understand the impact of their choices."

—Mandi Olson
Instructional Coach, Alpine School District
American Fork, UT

"Our current situation has created stressful challenges and uncertainties that could jeopardize our well-being as educators. Added expectations have shifted our attention away from our mission as educators—student learning. DeWitt provides a clear and evidence-based process to make us highly selective about what we bring into our schools."

—Caroline Picard
Former Assistant Superintendent for the Francophone School District, British Columbia, Canada
Education Consultant - Leadership & Coaching
Roberts Creek, BC, Canada

"De-implementation challenges schools to sharpen their focus and 'de-clutter' what has not made an impact by using a cycle of de-implementation. DeWitt offers practical examples and internal professional learning opportunities at the end of each chapter to help schools adopt a shared language for supporting improvement in their contexts."

—Helen Butler
CEO of Partners in Learning
Sunbury, Vic, Australia

"Peter M. DeWitt has a habit of leaping ahead avoiding tinkering and focusing on a substantial change agenda. Fortunately, he also insists on making the reader an action partner. There are five great ideas; and five stops along the way. Each time, you have a 'clutter check' where you clean up before you proceed. *De-implementation* is a book that helps you de-tox your change agenda, replacing it with a healthy streamlined focus on what really works."

—Michael Fullan
Professor Emeritus, Change Consultant and Author
Toronto, ON, Canada

De-implementation

De-implementation

Creating the Space to Focus on What Works

Peter M. DeWitt

Foreword by Andreas Schleicher

FOR INFORMATION

Corwin
A SAGE Company
2455 Teller Road
Thousand Oaks, California 91320
(800) 233-9936
www.corwin.com

SAGE Publications Ltd.
1 Oliver's Yard
55 City Road
London EC1Y 1SP
United Kingdom

SAGE Publications India Pvt. Ltd.
B 1/I 1 Mohan Cooperative Industrial Area
Mathura Road, New Delhi 110 044
India

SAGE Publications Asia-Pacific Pte. Ltd.
18 Cross Street #10-10/11/12
China Square Central
Singapore 048423

Clutter Check icon courtesy of iStock.com/ LueratSatichob.

Printed in Canada

ISBN 978-1-0718-8521-5

President: Mike Soules
President and Editorial Director: Monica Eckman
Senior Acquisitions Editor: Tanya Ghans
Content Development Manager: Desirée A. Bartlett
Editorial Assistant: Nyle De Leon
Project Editor: Amy Schroller
Copy Editor: Megan Speer-Levi
Typesetter: Hurix Digital
Cover Designer: Janet Kiesel
Marketing Manager: Morgan Fox

This book is printed on acid-free paper.

MIX
Paper from
responsible sources
FSC® C103567

22 23 24 25 26 10 9 8 7 6 5 4 3 2 1

Contents

Foreword

We all know that without substantial change, the gap between what education systems provide and what our societies demand is likely to widen further. There is a risk that education becomes our next steel industry, and schools a relic of the past. But to transform schooling at scale, we need not just a radical, alternative vision of what is needed and what is possible, but also smarter strategies that help make change in education happen.

Educators face tough choices when evaluating policy alternatives; they need to weigh the potential impact against the economic and political cost of change. Should they pursue what is most technically feasible? What is most politically and socially feasible? What can be implemented quickly? What can be sustainable over a sufficient time horizon? Even where we have all the answers, the reality is that the road of educational reform is littered with many good ideas that were poorly implemented.

One reason for the difficulty in reforming education is simply the scale and reach of the sector. Another is the laws, regulations, structures, and institutions on which policymakers tend to focus. They are just the small visible tip of a huge iceberg. The reason why it is so hard to move education systems is that there is a much larger, invisible part under the waterline. This invisible part is composed of the interests, beliefs, motivations, and fears of the people who are involved. Policymakers are rarely successful with education reform unless they help people recognize what needs to change, and build a shared understanding and collective ownership for change.

The potential loss of advantages or privileged positions also plays a role in education because the vast structure of established providers means that there are extensive vested interests. As a result, the status quo has many protectors—stakeholders in education who stand to lose a degree of power or influence if changes are made. It is difficult to ask the frogs to clear the swamp. Then there is often uncertainty about who will benefit from reforms and to what extent. Assessing the relative costs and benefits of reform in education is also difficult because of the large number of intervening factors that can influence the nature, size, and distribution of any improvements. The investment may be expensive over the long term, while in the short term it is rarely possible to predict clear, identifiable results from new policies, especially given the time lags between implementation and effect.

Timing is also relevant to education reform, and in more than one sense. Most significantly, there is a substantial gap between the time at which the initial cost of reform is incurred and the time when it is evident whether the benefits of reform will materialize. While timing complicates the politics of reform in many domains, it seems to have a greater impact on education reform, where the lags often involve many years. Policymakers may lose an election over education issues, but they rarely win an election because of education reform. That may also be why, across OECD countries, only about one in ten reforms is followed by any attempt to evaluate its impact.

But the elephant in the room is something else; it is the inability of education systems to unlearn and relearn when the context changes, which leads to students learning a mile wide but just an inch deep and educators getting entangled in complex administrative processes that nobody understands and takes real ownership of. I learned that lesson when designing the first PISA mathematics assessment. When studying national mathematics curricula for the development of our assessment as a starting point, I often asked myself why curricula devote as much attention to teaching things like trigonometry. When asking mathematicians, psychologists, and engineers, they determined that trigonometry was just one specific application of mathematics, was nowhere in the critical path of building conceptual understanding in mathematics, and that those skills had long been digitized and automated. Unfortunately, our school systems were unable to identify and get rid of things that became irrelevant.

This is where DeWitt's *De-implementation: Creating the Space to Focus on What Works* comes in. While numerous scholars have reviewed de-implementation processes, this is the most comprehensive and systematic attempt to understand de-implementation processes and to leverage this understanding to help educational practitioners and policymakers pursue fewer things at greater depth and take to heart that we do not need to do everything differently to do some things better.

—Andreas Schleicher
Director for Education and Skills and
Special Advisor on Education Policy to the Secretary-General
at the Organisation for Economic Co-operation and
Development (OECD), Paris

Acknowledgments

I would like to thank John Hattie and Arran Hamilton for engaging with me around this idea of de-implementation. The conversations have been very valuable.

No author writes a book alone, and I could not have written this one without the important and deep feedback offered by my editor, Tanya Ghans. As we know, it was kind of a rough time while I wrote this book, and you provided a light that kept me going. Thank you to Helen Butler, Stacy Storey, Tom Guskey, and Ray Boyd for the conversations on the topic of de-implementation, and for the friendship. And thank you to Andreas Schleicher for his important and impactful foreword.

During the writing of this book, I developed a partnership with Mike Nelson, Chris Beals, and Tom Murphy from the Washington Association of School Administrators (WASA). Along with Jenni Donohoo as my co-lead advisor for our work with Directors of Teaching and Learning, we not only formed a great team but became friends as well. Thank you for all the conversations.

Last, to my family: I'm better because of all of you.

About the Author

Peter M. DeWitt, EdD is a former K–5 teacher (eleven years) and principal (eight years). He is a school leadership coach who runs competency-based workshops and provides keynotes nationally and internationally, focusing on school leadership (collaborative cultures and instructional leadership), as well as fostering inclusive school climates.

Additionally, Peter coaches school-based leaders, directors, instructional coaches, teacher leaders, and school-based leadership teams both in person and remotely. In summer 2021 Peter created a yearlong on-demand asynchronous coaching course through Thinkific where he has fostered a community of learners that includes K–12 educators in leadership positions.

Peter's work has been adopted at the state and university level, and he works with numerous school districts, school boards, regional networks, and ministries of education around North America, Australia, Europe, Asia, the Middle East, and the UK.

Peter writes the "Finding Common Ground" column for *Education Week*, which has been in circulation since 2011. In 2020 Peter co-created *Education Week*'s "A Seat at the Table" series, where he moderates conversations with experts around the topics of race, gender, sexual orientation, research, trauma, and many other educational topics.

Additionally, Peter is the editor for the Connected Educator series (Corwin) and the Impact series (Corwin), which include books by Viviane Robinson, Andy Hargreaves, Pasi Sahlberg, Yong Zhao, and Michael Fullan. He is the 2013 School Administrators

Association of New York State's (SAANYS) Outstanding Educator of the Year and the 2015 Education Blogger of the Year (Academy of Education Arts & Sciences), and he sits on numerous advisory boards. Peter is the author, co-author, or contributor of numerous books, including the following:

- *Dignity for All: Safeguarding LGBT Students* (Corwin, 2012)

- *School Climate Change* (co-authored with Sean Slade; ASCD, 2014)

- *Flipping Leadership Doesn't Mean Reinventing the Wheel* (Corwin, 2014)

- *Collaborative Leadership: Six Influences That Matter Most* (Corwin/Learning Forward, 2016)

- *School Climate: Leading With Collective Teacher Efficacy* (Corwin/Ontario Principals Council, 2017)

- *Coach It Further: Using the Art of Coaching to Improve School Leadership* (Corwin, 2018)

- *Instructional Leadership: Creating Practice Out of Theory* (Corwin, 2020)

- *10 Mindframes for Leaders: The Visible Learning Approach to School Success* (edited by John Hattie and Ray Smith; Corwin, 2020)

- *Collective Leader Efficacy: Strengthening the Impact of Instructional Leadership Teams* (Corwin/Learning Forward, 2021)

Peter's articles have appeared in educational research journals at the state, national, and international level. His books have been translated into four languages.

Some of the organizations Peter has worked with are the American Association of School Administrators (AASA), Arkansas State University, EDUTAS, University of Oklahoma, Victoria Department of Education (Australia), University of Rotterdam (Netherlands), Washington Association of School Administrators (WASA), Texas Association of School Administrators (TASA), the National Education Association (NEA), New Brunswick Teacher's Association (Canada), the National Association of Secondary School Principals (NASSP), Education Scotland (Scotland), Glasgow City Council (Scotland), Kuwait Technical College (Kuwait), the National Association of School Psychologists, ASCD, l'Association des directions et directions adjointes des écoles franco-ontariennes (ADFO), the Catholic Principals' Council of Ontario (CPCO), the Ontario Principals' Council (OPC), National School Climate Center, GLSEN, PBS, NPR, BAM Radio Network, ABC, and NBC's Education Nation.

To my mom, Gail DeWitt. 4/28/34–11/24/21

To Patricia (Trish) Choukeir. 5/2/64–3/31/22.
My sister. My protector. My best friend.
You always showed so much strength for all of us.

To Doug. Thanks for helping me breathe.

Introduction

Burn Out or Fade Away

We know that school leaders, as well as educators, students, and families around the world, have been through many challenges as a result of COVID-19. The reality is that those challenges have been daily, because of schedule changes, contact tracing, choosing from a disappearing list of substitute teachers to cover for a teacher out because of the virus, and a whole host of other crises that come up seemingly every hour.

Academic and social-emotional focus used to be for students, but over the past year, many schools have begun to understand that a balance between academics and social-emotional learning is for teachers and leaders too. There has been an increase in stress and anxiety, and it could have a devastating impact on our school communities if we do not change it. Leaders and teachers are burning out or in some cases fading away and leaving the profession.

This is not a new issue. This increase in stress and anxiety has been happening for the past couple of decades. In the United States, Levin et al. (2020) found that "42 percent of principals indicated they were considering leaving their position." According to the study, "Nationally, the average tenure of a principal is about four years, and nearly one in five principals, approximately 18 percent, turn over annually. Often the schools that need the most capable principals, those serving students from low-income families, have even greater principal turnover."

Queen and Schumacher (2006) found that "as many as 75 percent of principals experience stress-related symptoms that include fatigue, weakness, lack of energy, irritability, heartburn, headache, trouble sleeping, sexual dysfunction, and depression" (p. 18).

This is a worldwide issue. In fact, the *Australian Principal Occupational Health, Safety, and Wellbeing Survey 2017 Data* shows that one in three school principals are in serious distress and one in three principals have been exposed to physical violence (Riley, 2018).

Leaders are not alone in this crisis. Ninety-two percent of teachers in an *Education Week* study said they were more stressed out in fall 2021 than they were in fall 2020, before we had a vaccine.

The annual Teacher Wellbeing Index, which is published in the United Kingdom, found that 77 percent of teachers surveyed in 2021 experienced symptoms of poor mental health due to their work, and 54 percent of teachers surveyed considered leaving the sector in the past two years due to pressures on their mental health (Scanlan & Savill-Smith, 2022).

Even though we know these statistics, many school districts reply, "Yeah, but . . ." Yeah, we know people are burned out, but we must keep moving forward. This is not only ridiculous; it is negatively impacting the personal and professional lives of practitioners who have worked really hard to get there. We can't talk about mental health and do nothing to help alleviate the issues impacting mental health.

One of the biggest factors in educators' stress levels is the breadth of tasks they are juggling. Educators, like the rest of us, often chase shiny new ideas they may in fact not need. We must get off the hamster wheel of new initiatives to really understand whether what we are presently doing is working, and that is where de-implementation enters the equation.

Sharpening Our Focus by Working Together

Our focus in school should always be on student learning and the impact of teachers and leaders, as well as the students themselves, on that learning. That's a given. But which strategies will best help us have a deeper impact on student learning? Are they the practices we have been engaging in for a long time, or are they the fresher ideas we brainstormed together? Understanding what best impacts student learning requires adults within the school to learn from one another as well. Hattie and Yates (2014) say, "Human learning is a slow process that can happen over months and years rather than hours and days" (p. 113).

Hattie and Yates (2014) go on to say that for that learning to take place, "the necessary ingredients are (a) time, (b) goal-orientation, (c) supportive feedback, (d) accumulated successful practice, and (d) frequent review" (p. 113).

What does that have to do with de-implementation? Quite simply: everything. Teachers, staff, and school leaders need to spend time engaging in discussions about what practices successfully help impact student learning, and carefully decide which practices, on the part of both students and adults, need to stay and which ones need to go. Just to be clear, de-implementation is not about limiting the number of strategies we try in our classrooms and schools, but it is about knowing when to get rid of or replace the ones that aren't working.

Where It All Began

In early spring 2021, I was having separate conversations with Arran Hamilton from Cognition Education, based in New Zealand, and John Hattie from the University of Melbourne in Australia. They were partnering on some work involving de-implementation. Hattie sent me the medical field research on de-implementation, which began a few short years ago, and we began emailing back and forth because he suggested that I explore it too. During a rabbit-hole moment, where I found myself clicking on citations of citations of citations, I found research from the field of school psychology.

What I found out is the process of de-implementation is not new. In 1990, Drucker wrote, "The first policy—and the foundation for all the others—is to abandon yesterday. The first need is to free resources from being committed to maintaining what no longer contributes to performance and no longer produces results. In fact, it is not possible to create tomorrow unless one first sloughs off yesterday" (Drucker, 2018, p. 1).

Drucker went on to write, "Planned, purposeful abandonment of the old and of the unrewarding is a prerequisite to successful pursuit of the new and highly promising" (p. 2).

The goal of this book is to take the readers back to "that planned, purposeful abandonment," also referred to as de-implementation. Through slowing down and carefully curating the tools they use, schools can find their way back to balance.

How This Book Works

Within this book, I share the roots of the de-implementation research and how I have adapted it to fit educators' needs. These adaptations make the process of de-implementation less complex and easier to engage in as an individual or team. Each chapter includes real-life scenarios, "clutter checks" that provide a moment for you to pause and think about your current practices, activities, support for roadblocks, a bit of psychology to peer into how our minds help or hinder de-implementation, and tools or guiding questions to help you rally your focus around what works for your school community. This book will also signal where the process of de-implementing can be quick and when it will need to be more formal (see Chapter 4).

This book is based on some assumptions:

- Schools are places of learning, not just for students but for adults as well.

- Too often, the initiatives schools adopt arise from the ideas of a few instead of the collaborative thinking of many.

- The workload of teachers, staff, and leaders has increased over the past two decades, and it is time to partially reduce or replace some of the actions they take, for their mental health and well-being.

- To have a true impact on student and adult learning, schools need an intentional process to understand what is working and what is not.

- There are school leaders in this world who will give teachers and leaders permission to do this work.

I want you to really engage with this text. Highlight it, mark it up, add your epiphanies, and most important, work with your team. A key premise of this work is that it can be successful only if key members of the community have a say in the decision-making process.

Last, the focus should always be how de-implementation will lead to a greater impact on student learning. I believe that de-implementation is a concept school leaders and teachers must explore. Make no mistake though: this process is all about professional learning. When your team—however many people make up that team—engages in the de-implementation process, it is meant to be an impactful form of professional learning.

Le Fevre et al. (2019, pp. 7–8) suggest that there are six important roots to facilitating professional learning:

1. Adopting an evaluative inquiry stance—De-implementation is based in inquiry and evaluation.

2. Valuing and using deep conceptual knowledge—This book asks you to position yourself as a learner and look at the bigger picture of how, within all of what you do, you impact student learning.

3. Being agentic—It is important that every person who does this work feels a sense of agency to use their most authentic voices.

4. Being aware of cultural positioning—Le Fevre et al. (2019) say that "cultural positioning is about the way people experience the world through specific cultural lenses" (p. 25).

5. Being metacognitive—All of you must have a deep understanding about your own level of thinking and reasoning.

6. Bringing a systemic focus—No matter how small you start with the de-implementation process, you must see how it will help improve the greater system you teach and lead in.

So before you continue reading the book, I'm asking that you engage in your first activity, which is about your beliefs when it comes to student learning and school. Brandt and Sleegers (2021) define an individual's belief system as "a network of causally connected attitudes and identities" (p. 159). Below, you will need to consider your beliefs about student learning. The following are the steps I want you to take for this activity:

Regardless of whether you are engaging in this book as a partnership or group, I would like you to first fill it out by yourself.

1. Write down three beliefs you have about learning, students, or education. These are three beliefs that you would defend to anyone.

2. If you are working with a partner or team, share your three beliefs. During the process of sharing beliefs, be willing to question the beliefs of others and be open to having them question your beliefs.

3. Take time to write down the relevant actions you engage in that ultimately assist you in your three beliefs. Many times, people won't write down management-type activities because they don't think those can be relevant to achieving their beliefs, but I think some management techniques do help us achieve our beliefs.

4. Take time to write down the distractions that may prevent you from achieving those beliefs.

As you engage with this book, I want you to come back to your beliefs, as well as the relevant actions and distractions, with your team. During the time you read this book and engage in the activities, take time to notice whether any of your beliefs evolve or change.

My purpose is to set the precedent at the beginning that I really want this process to be well thought out and human. Engaging in conversations with one another around an idea can lead to some of our best professional development. Books should never be part of a process done to you but should be part of a process done with you that includes your voice.

Peter M. DeWitt, EdD

What Are Educators Interested in De-implementing?

In a survey of educators and school leaders from all parts of the world, the following are some of the areas they said they would like to de-implement in one way, shape, or form. Some of the ideas are followed by quotations from the survey.

Meetings—This is by far the most popular area for people to begin. They have a meeting to establish the agenda for another meeting, and then they have a meeting after the meeting to discuss it all!

Email—Educators are burned out when it comes to checking email. Although you won't have to go through a cycle of de-implementation to minimize how often people check email, it is an area that comes up a lot in workshops and coaching.

Drive-by professional development—Teachers, school psychologists, counselors, and leaders are minimizing the time they spend in one-time professional development and instead are engaging in community-of-learners practice that evolves over a number of months or years.

Top-down professional development—Educators would like to replace top-down district-run professional development with professional learning that is based on the needs of teachers and students!

PowerPoint—"Replace PowerPoint lessons with thinking routines and inquiry learning. Students can engage in deeper learning through self-discovery and research than when fed content from a PowerPoint."

In-school-only learning—For many reasons, including what we discovered during COVID-19, teachers and leaders understand that students learn outside the classroom as much as, if not more than, they learn in the classroom. Those teachers and leaders have replaced an in-school-learning-only mindset with one that understands a great deal of learning takes place in a social context within and outside of school.

Teacher talk—"Too much teacher talk—replace with engaging student talk; the person talking is doing the learning."

Zero tolerance policies—This form of discipline has been seen to be not only harmful but also discriminatory.

Homework—Educators are de-implementing homework in a variety of ways, meaning that they are trying to partially reduce the amount of homework they give to students, or replacing their usual homework with the opportunity for students to engage in passion projects.

Child Study Team (CST) process—Teams want to replace the deficit mindset that often comes with this process with one that focuses on strengths as well as weaknesses.

Special education practices—Schools want to replace special education with a more human and strengths-based process to maximize the opportunities for students with exceptionalities.

Biased or one-sided historical content—The year 2021 was unprecedented when it came to backlash against teaching a more diverse and realistic history. De-implementation in this area means making sure that our historical content in school focuses on a more well-balanced approach and an unabashedly true depiction of history.

The Trouble With Implementation

(and how to make it better)

1

Right now, no agenda is shared before the meeting and no minutes are taken during/after the meeting. I would reverse that. Meetings will have more impact if you have the agenda beforehand, and we should take minutes to reflect and move on to the next steps that were decided.

—Anonymous

SUCCESS CRITERIA

By the end of this chapter, you will be able to identify the following:

- Why we have a need to over-implement

- How we can improve implementation

- Five questions to help guide your implementation

- How to overcome our overconsumption mindset

Add two of your own success criteria:

-

-

We are a world consumed with overconsumption. We are consistently hit with messages that we need new things to make us happy. When I was growing up, we lived in a house that our mom and dad built in

1959. Over the twenty years we lived in that house, which we recently sold after my mom passed, we had one green rotary phone hanging on the wall. Nowadays, the message is that we need to upgrade our phones every single year. We sit back and watch as others entertain us.

To some it is called progress, but to others it is called overconsumption. We passively consume curriculum, content, technology tools, and words at meetings as if we are playing the supporting role in our own lives. What makes it worse is that we consume because we have the fear of missing out (FOMO), so we begin to rally our troops in the war of overconsumption. This combination of FOMO and our need to consume new things contributes to why we over-implement and leads to the anxiety and exhaustion we feel.

What we all need is time to focus and cut down on the noise. We need time to breathe and engage in conversations that focus on deeper impact. We need time to feel inspired, time when we can curate new ideas and look for teachable moments, but we won't get that time back until we begin taking some things off our plates.

CASE IN POINT

The "More Is More" Philosophy

In my work, I coach school leaders and teams, facilitate workshops, and provide keynotes, both nationally and internationally. When I first began doing this work, I had lots of content that I felt I needed to cover. I had the "more is more" philosophy. For a full-day workshop I had at least a hundred slides. At the end of the day, my voice was raw from talking so much. But it took a road trip with colleagues to bring this into sharp relief.

A few years ago, I began working in partnership with the University of Oklahoma with several colleagues, facilitating sessions that included principals and assistant principals.

My colleagues and I would drive one hour and fifteen minutes to the venue, and during the car ride we would talk about the content for the day, even though we had already had a video call about it. At the venue, we would meet with the four coaches responsible for coaching participants within the group, and then I would meet with participants to facilitate the learning. At the end of the six-and-a-half-hour session, my colleagues and I would meet with the coaches for one hour to go over the pluses and deltas for the day. Then we would get in the car for our hour-and-fifteen-minute drive back to the hotel, during which one of us read all the feedback out loud in detail. That was more than five hours of meeting for one session, which began to feel . . . excessive. However, during one of these car meetings, an important nugget of truth came out about how much *doing* I was doing during my sessions.

As we were driving back to the hotel, one of my colleagues asked me if I knew the ratio of my talking versus participants' talking. I said it was split evenly. I was wrong. I would speak for thirty minutes and give participants ten minutes to speak. I was consistently more concerned about covering content. I was hitting participants with everything, including the kitchen sink, because I felt that the more I gave them, the more they would see me as a credible source. This lined up with the written feedback I was getting from participants. While the audience noted that the information was great and I knew my stuff, some people wrote that they needed time to process. I thought they meant they needed to process it after they left, but what they really needed was for me to slow down so they could think during the session.

Upon reflection, our team worked to streamline our meeting time, and I changed the way I ran workshops. I still have the same time allotted as I did, but now I develop success criteria with the audience, talk for ten to fifteen minutes, and give them ten to fifteen minutes to process. And I took out a bunch of slides that did not matter. The result was more time for creative thinking and workshops that produced deeper conversations than ever before.

What are your thoughts on overconsumption in your personal life?

Do you have concerns about overconsumption within your school?

For those of you who are district leaders, how has overconsumption impacted you?

CLUTTER CHECK

Educational Trends Over the Past Thirty Years

In the following chart, you will find a list of popular educational trends over the past thirty years or so. These educational trends are not just from the United States, because they have been found in and have impacted other countries as well. Take a moment to read through the list, and even add to it. This list has been broken up into the broad categories of districtwide/schoolwide, classroom, and leadership practices.

DISTRICTWIDE/ SCHOOLWIDE INITIATIVES AND PROGRAMS	CLASSROOM PRACTICES AND STRATEGIES	LEADERSHIP PRACTICES AND STRATEGIES
Open classrooms	Fixed grouping/flexible grouping	No Child Left Behind
Standards-based bulletin boards	Lectures/student talk	Building management
D.A.R.E.	Turn and talk	Professional learning communities (PLCs)
Portfolios	Jigsaw	Evaluations (Danielson, Focused Teacher Evaluation Model)
Project-based learning	DEAR time	Walkthroughs
Whole word versus phonics	Popcorn reading	Staff meetings
Packaged programs (Houghton-Mifflin, Scholastic, Readers and Writers Workshop)	Extrinsic behavior incentive charts (red, yellow, green; ClassDojo)	Schoolwide professional development
Running records	Sound walls	One-on-ones
Multiple intelligences	Flexible seating	Japanese lesson study
Bloom's taxonomy	Journaling	Differentiated supervision
Social-emotional learning	Understanding by Design	Snapshot feedback
Trauma-informed instruction	Small-group instruction	Instructional leadership
Leveled texts	Conferencing	Distributive leadership
Site-based professional development	Decodable texts	Site-based decision models
Social justice curriculum	Independent reading	Advanced certification
I-Ready	PowerPoint lessons	Various leadership standards
MAP assessments	Reading skills/strategies	Well-being leadership
Smartboards	Building knowledge	Look-fors
Blended learning	Correcting student work/ not correcting student work	Transparent/publicly shared data
Personalized learning	Daily homework/no homework	Instructional rounds
Math Talk	Exit slips	Transformational leadership
Common Core	Cold-calling	Community schools
High-stakes testing	Whole-class novels/ individual texts	Collective leadership
Singapore math	Direct/constructivist instruction	Leading for equity
Inquiry-based science	Socratic methods	Leading like a coach

The point here is not to evaluate the merit of each; hopefully, by the end of this book you will do that work yourself. It is to show that quite a lot has been created and implemented—with varying degrees of research support. Notice that often, concurrent trends were diametrically opposed to each other. Furthermore, some of these ideas, particularly those in the left column, can take a lot of time to implement effectively, often years.

The question becomes, how does a school district or individual school know where to devote its resources? For example, if you are a new leader and your data tells you that 65 percent of your student population is reading below grade level, this may not be the year to introduce project-based learning (that is, if the research shows it is a worthwhile endeavor; again, no judgment at this point). But for so many leaders there is this well-intentioned desire to give their children what they think is best for them all at once. One goal of this text is to help us all decelerate and reflect so we are making wise and informed choices. It is also to give educators the permission to say no to ideas that do not support their goals. More can be more, but often more is simply too much.

The list above is just a fraction of the trends we have seen in education around the world. On a separate sheet of paper, brainstorm different initiatives your school has started over the past few years. After you write your list, circle the ones that are still left. What does this have to do with de-implementation? Imagine all the time you or your team spent on initiatives that didn't last. If you didn't engage in them in the first place, think of the time you would get back.

CLUTTER
CHECK

Five Reasons We Over-Implement

This chapter will share a plan for improving implementation, but first I thought it worthwhile to share some of the reasons we educators tend to over-implement. It is important to think about these causes because knowing them can help us identify them when they are happening. This awareness can help us all pump the breaks or interrupt patterns that feed educational hoarding.

1) Thin Content in Nice Packaging

Many of the programs we chase after claim to be evidence-based when they are not. Take, for instance, the assertion that many products make about being tied to brain science. In fact, when it comes to programs that claim to be brain-based, Craig et al. (2021) recently wrote,

"Brain images significantly impact lay readers' belief in the veracity of the findings; McCabe and Castel (2008) found that individuals incorrectly rated findings as scientifically meritorious when brain images were included than when only text was provided" (p. 128). So basically, organizations would place an image of a brain to promote it being brain-based when it really wasn't, and educators were more likely to choose the program not tied to brain research just because of the image.

Research also shows that teachers, district leaders, and building leaders do not always vet what they use in their classrooms, districts, or school buildings. Craig et al. (2021) go on to write,

> Pinterest is one vehicle that teachers commonly use to quickly and easily find and curate curriculum, lesson plans, and other educational ideas. Teachers report that Pinterest is among the top five websites they use for professional development, and education-related pins are the second most highly searched type of pin (Schroeder et al., 2019), with 87% of elementary teachers and 62% of secondary teachers reporting that they use Pinterest for math resources (Hu et al., 2018). (p. 129)

This does not mean teachers and leaders should stop using Pinterest. What it does mean is that teachers need to assess more of the ideas they like on Pinterest by finding a piece of valid research that supports the use of the strategy.

This has another side to it as well. I have found that district leaders, building leaders, and teachers get caught up in *who* is offering the nice packaging. What I mean here is that speakers who give keynotes and facilitate workshops come out with new material, and some educators blindly follow one speaker because they always like what that speaker has to offer. Like buying a favorite rock band's new album, educators want to pick it up and use it without even taking time to question whether they need it.

Yes, I understand the irony of writing that as an author and speaker. Educators come to my workshops, and I always appreciate that they want to connect and learn, because I often learn from them as well. However, over the past couple of years, I have been intentional in asking audiences whether what I am offering is what they need. Don't do it because I am offering practices grounded in research; do it because what I am offering is what your school or district needs. We all have a responsibility in overconsumption.

2) Emotions Over Evidence

Educators are human, and humans get attached to things. It is very hard to part with things we like, even when we find out they're ineffective or harmful. Below are four examples of common areas where educators' practices and the research are misaligned.

Zero Tolerance Policies

School districts are beginning to change their stance on zero tolerance policies and adopt more equitable discipline policies, but not everyone within a school agrees with that change. There are staff within schools, and proponents outside of schools, who strongly want to see all students disciplined and believe that zero tolerance policies are the best way to do that. However, the American Psychological Association Zero Tolerance Task Force (2008) writes,

> An extensive review of the literature found that, despite a 20-year history of implementation, there are surprisingly few data that could directly test the assumptions of a zero tolerance approach to school discipline, and the data that are available tend to contradict those assumptions. Moreover, zero tolerance policies may negatively affect the relationship of education with juvenile justice and appear to conflict to some degree with current best knowledge concerning adolescent development. (p. 1)

MSV (the Three-Cueing System)

A few months ago, I was doing a series of webinars for the Universal Early Literacy Program, which is a part of the NYC Department of Education. During one of the webinars, we focused on de-implementation, and I asked participants what they would de-implement. Many responded on the topic of using meaning, syntax, and visual prompts to support students while doing running records in a K–2 setting. The coaches accurately stated that the science of reading does not support using these cues; "encouraging kids to check the picture when they come to a tricky word, or to hypothesize what word would work in the sentence, can take their focus away from the word itself—lowering the chances that they'll use their understanding of letter sounds to read through the word part-by-part, and be able to recognize it more quickly the next time they see it" (Schwartz, 2020).

I asked what they would replace running records that focused on miscues with, and we got into a deep discussion on phonemic awareness activities that would be more impactful. However, a few people spoke

"It is very hard to part with things we like, even when we find out they're ineffective or harmful."

up and said, "But we really believe in this method!" The sense of loss was palpable, and at that moment evidence wasn't enough.

Butterflies

Let's take a quick look at the example of butterflies. Yes, butterflies. For years when I was a principal, our staff had a conversation about what we could stop doing in our classes as part of a great school alignment of curriculum. Butterflies were taught in three different years, with essentially the same content, but no one wanted to stop focusing on butterflies, because they liked doing it.

Professional Learning Communities

Here is one more example, but this one works a bit in the reverse. Data shows that professional learning communities (PLCs) are effective, and wildly popular with leaders; so on that score, implementing them makes sense. However, citing a Boston Consulting Group Study (2014), Hargreaves and O'Connor (2018) write,

> Professional learning communities (PLCs) were one of the most disliked forms of professional development among surveyed teachers, even though providers and administrators were highly supportive of the approach. . . . A given PLC model may seem to offer a promising blueprint for collective inquiry and shared decision making. But if teachers see it as (just another) reform imposed on them from above, then they'll likely experience it as such. The protocols and terminology may be new, but they'll grumble about being forced, yet again, to go through the motions of meeting with each other, agreeing on group norms, defining shared goals, and so on. (p. 21)

The issue here is about how PLCs are being implemented. Based on this research, teachers view this as something being done to them, which is rarely an effective strategy. If PLCs are to be effective, then teacher voice is a must.

3) Time Mismanagement

Time is the next challenge to proper implementation. This section will focus on meetings, which are an international phenomenon, because again and again, meetings of all types are the offender in time mismanagement. The reasons for this often boil down to redundancy, imbalance of topics, and the erosion of focus.

Like zero tolerance policies, running records using three cues, or butterfly curriculum, we all have one activity or initiative we value. What is one you value?

CLUTTER
CHECK

Activity/initiative you value_____

What is one piece of evidence you could collect to understand how it's working? _____
_____

What is one piece of evidence you could collect to understand that it's not working? _____
_____
_____

Redundancy—This often happens when planning is reactionary and there is poor communication among key stakeholders. Add to that the fact that teachers may not feel comfortable saying they have already received information, and you have created the perfect storm for redundancy.

Imbalance of topics—The other day I was at a weekly curriculum meeting with a group of directors, building leaders, and instructional coaches. Everyone spoke about how they wanted to focus on student learning, and most people left the meeting feeling refreshed. Yet people were concerned the curriculum meeting would revert to old habits and focus only on reacting to a crisis or some other issue that the district felt took priority. It's not to say those issues were not important, but the problem was that they were not balanced with a focus on student learning. In surveying staff, there was time for both, but the challenges took over the learning.

Erosion of focus—The previous example dovetails with this issue of focus erosion. This means that a meeting that was earmarked for one thing over time has shifted into something else. In the worst-case scenario, venting and complaining may take up an inordinate amount of time. Or participants use the meeting time to take care of other important work. These outcomes are often due to ineffective planning, misunderstanding of participants' needs, or continuing something out of habit rather than purpose.

4) Workaholic Cultures

When it comes to school culture, Gruenert (2008) writes, "Whenever a group of people spend a significant amount of time together, they develop a common set of expectations. These expectations evolve into unwritten rules to which group members conform in order to remain in good standing with their colleagues" (p. 57).

Over the years, I have heard school districts state that they care about mental health and well-being. However, some of these same school leaders expect teachers and building leaders to check email at night before they go to bed, work on Saturdays to engage in professional learning, or offer Saturday school for their students who are failing. Their culture rewards working long hours and focusing on many initiatives, even if it means becoming a martyr to get there.

I remember a superintendent who told his principals they should stop complaining because "those principals get paid a good salary and they should shut up and do their damn job." He left a year later, but not before several of his principals moved to different school districts and the teachers and students they left behind got their next round of principals.

5) Initiatives We Can't Control

Most people will agree that there are too many top-down initiatives in education and that they exacerbate the problem of over-implementation. In countless surveys that I did during workshops and keynotes focusing on this work, the number one area teachers and leaders said we should de-implement is high-stakes testing. In fact, one time I was giving a keynote for school leaders from across the state of Arkansas, and the room also had many legislators there as well, and high-stakes testing came up in the anonymous survey because the leaders in the room wanted to send a message to their legislature.

Here's the issue: we can be outspoken about high-stakes testing and its lack of merit (Farvis & Hay, 2020), but we can't always get caught up in it within our own buildings and districts because it takes us away from the other work we could be doing. Don't get me wrong: I was one of eight principals in New York State who wrote a letter to the State Education Department asserting that high-stakes testing should not be tied to teacher evaluation, but I also knew I needed to focus on the things I could control.

Improving Implementation

We have spent the beginning of this chapter illuminating how and where implementation can go awry. Now let's shift to how to implement better. Yes, this book is about de-implementation, but in many ways, it is also about how we implement in the first place. First some information about the implementation science.

The Science

Grant (2016) writes, "It's widely assumed that there's a tradeoff between quantity and quality—if you want to do better work, you have to do less of it—but this turns out to be false" (p. 37). So where do fresh ideas, the need to keep old ones, and implementation interconnect? It begins with the science of implementation.

Nilsen et al. (2020) suggest, "The birth of implementation science is usually linked to the emergence of evidence-based medicine and practice in the 1990s" (p. 2).

They go on to suggest there are five categories of theoretical approaches used in implementation science (p. 3):

- Process models
- Determinant frameworks
- Classic theories
- Implementation theories
- Evaluation frameworks

What I am offering to readers here is a process model or, more specifically, a planned action model. Nilsen et al. (2020) say,

> Planned action models are process models that facilitate implementation by offering practical guidance in the planning and execution of implementation endeavours and/or implementation strategies. Action models elucidate important aspects that need to be considered in implementation practice and usually prescribe a number of stages or steps that should be followed in the process of translating research into practice. (p. 4)

In reviewing numerous implementation models, I came across one that I feel fits well for implementation. It's referred to as the Practical, Robust Implementation and Sustainability Model, also known as PRISM.

A Model for Implementation

Feldstein and Glasgow (2008) write, "A conceptual framework for improving practice is needed to integrate the key features for successful

"Yes, this book is about de-implementation, but in many ways, it is also about how we implement in the first place."

program design, predictors of program implementation success, factors associated with diffusion and maintenance, and appropriate outcome measures" (p. 228).

They go on to write that their "primary focus is the health care practice, but the model is also applicable to other settings where health interventions may be delivered, such as work sites or school-based settings." When thinking of adaptation, we should consider that this level of implementation has implications regardless of whether we live in Australia, the Netherlands, or the United States.

So let's take some time to look at PRISM. I have adapted it to fit the educational needs of good implementation.

PRISM

The intervention, or the new initiative under consideration, is first broken into two main categories: the organizational perspective and the organizational characteristics. Each is considered from both the staff and student perspective, taking into account Senge's principles that focus on systems thinking and building a shared vision. Schools cannot have a shared vision if they do not account for and understand the perspective and characteristics of their community. These are then followed by additional elements that need to be taken into consideration. See Figure 1.1, followed by an explanation of each part.

Organizational Perspective

Staff perspective—What does a proper implementation of strategies and programs mean for the organization? How will leaders, teachers, and staff support it, and how will it help them be more impactful? Please remember when considering staff and student perspectives, this is not just building based but needs to be considered for district initiatives as well.

Student perspective—Many schools have been approaching the student perspective by using surveys. However, empathy interviews are a growing trend for many school leaders and teachers. Empathy interviews take into consideration cultural perspectives of students, as well as those students with exceptional abilities. Example questions:

- How do you feel you best learn in the classroom?

- What makes learning difficult/challenging for you?

- What strategies do I use in the classroom as a teacher that help you understand the content better?

Figure 1.1

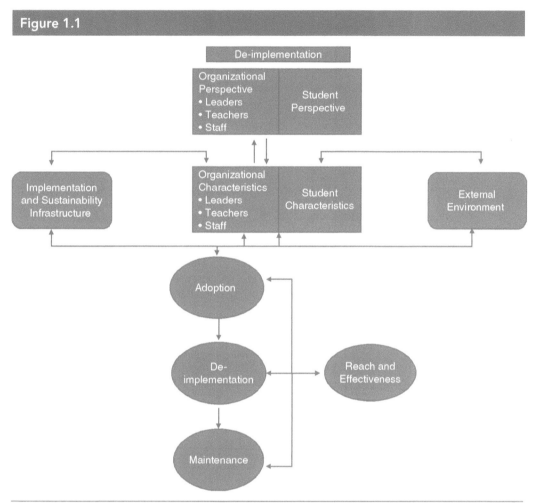

Adapted from: Feldstein, A.C., Glasgow, RE (2008). A Practical, Robust Implementation and Sustainability Model (PRISM) for Integrating Research Findings into Practice. The Joint Commission Journal on Quality and Patient Safety.

Organizational Characteristics

Staff characteristics—What characteristics of the organization help support the work or become a barrier to getting the work done? Issues of funding or high turnover rate of leaders and teachers may be two such barriers.

Student characteristics—How have the characteristics of students been considered when it comes to the implementation of new initiatives? Example considerations:

- Different modalities needed in the learning process that account for both those students who can immediately participate and those who need time to reflect before they participate

- Knowledge dimensions, like factual, procedural, conceptual, and metacognitive (Anderson & Krathwohl, 2001)

Understanding the perspectives and characteristics of our stakeholders is important, because if we lack that understanding, our ideas will often fail.

Implementation and sustainability infrastructure—A shared conviction that an instructional leadership team can have a positive impact on student learning (DeWitt, 2021). That is part of the infrastructure that we must consider to do the work of implementation.

External environment—How much support do schools get from their boards of education or their school community?

Adoption—How will this work get adopted? What are the reasons for adopting this particular initiative? How will this initiative help our school community improve? In what ways will our school roll it out?

Implementation—Are instructional leadership teams using a structured approach to implement new initiatives? (See cycle of de-implementation and program logic model in Chapters 4 and 5 as examples.) Does that cycle of de-implementation focus on having a positive impact on student learning? Or is it about making adults work harder on things that may not have impact at all?

Maintenance—Maintenance means taking time each month during faculty meetings, PLC meetings, or department meetings to focus on the program. Every initiative must include maintenance. Too often schools implement and never provide follow-up professional learning about the strategies and program.

Implementing an initiative or new idea is not like posting on social media. You can't just do it once and hope that people will like it, follow it, or reshare it. It requires maintenance.

Reach and effectiveness—What evidence is being collected to understand the reach and impact of the strategies and program?

If you are thinking that is a lot of work, think of the time and money spent on the resources and training for a program only for it to be partially implemented. If school and district teams went through this process every time, they would probably make better choices when it comes to what they implement.

In the Clutter Check that follows, we are going to take the perspective and characteristic sections from PRISM and perform a temperature check to get an understanding of where your school or district is in those two areas. Although each prompt says, "In this school . . ." districts can replace the word *school* with *district*.

"Implementing an initiative or new idea is not like posting on social media. You can't just do it once and hope that people will like it, follow it, or reshare it. It requires maintenance."

1. In this school, we carefully consider initiatives before we implement them.

   1   5

CLUTTER CHECK

2. In this school, teacher voices are valued in the decision-making process before initiatives are implemented.

   1   5

3. In this school, we focus our efforts as much on what can be taken off our plates as on what we need to put on our plates.

   1   5

4. In this school, mental health and well-being are not just talked about, but we also take actionable steps to alleviate the stress we feel.

   1   5

5. In this school, leaders have a voice in the decision-making process before initiatives are implemented.

   1   5

6. In this school, student voices are considered before initiatives are implemented.

   1   5

7. In this school, our initiatives are learner focused.

   1   5

8. In this school, learning is the focus of our mission and vision statements, and we can list several ways we are intentional with this focus.

   1   5

A Quick Guide for Good Implementation

In a private communication, Tom Guskey, an assessment, grading, and self-efficacy researcher and expert, sent me six questions he has found helpful in better implementation. You will see these again later in the book, because they will also help us in the de-implementation process. These questions partner well with PRISM when considering Senge's principles of developing systems thinking, creating a shared vision, and engaging in team learning. In the table below are the six questions along with some commentary to help you go deeper.

What are the specific goals of the program?	What are you hoping to accomplish through this initiative? What will you gain within this specific focus? How will this program empower people?
How valuable or important are those goals?	Are those goals worth implementing yet another initiative in your school or classroom? Are they focused on student learning?
What evidence would you trust to verify those goals were met?	What evidence will you collect to understand successful implementation?
Would all stakeholders in the program trust the same evidence?	Teachers, leaders, and students often trust different evidence.
How soon would you expect to attain that evidence?	Guskey has said in the past that teachers want to see that a strategy works within weeks and not months.
How much "improvement" is sufficient (cost-effectiveness)?	How does this implementation lead to improvement? Has it been cost-effective?

Addressing Our Assumptions

To do this work, leaders and their teams need to address the assumptions they have in a few different areas. Assumptions are things we believe to be true or effective without looking at the evidence to see if that is so. Senge (1990) refers to this phenomenon as mental models. He writes, "Mental models are deeply ingrained assumptions, generalizations, or even pictures or images that influence how we understand the world or how we take action" (p. 8). Schools are places where so many different assumptions are happening simultaneously.

For example, when the Common Core State Standards were being adopted, there was pushback from teachers, leaders, and parents in certain states across the United States. It got to the point that people hated it so much that they held deep assumptions that anything related to the Common Core was bad and needed to be dumped. The reality is that there were valuable parts to the Common Core too, but negative assumptions clouded the judgment of those educators who didn't like it.

As we go through the process, those conversations about assumptions will be vital. It's important to remember that it's not as much about what we like and don't like as it is about what practices are low value and what practices add value to the impact we are trying to have on student learning.

Some of these assumptions are as follows:

- There is one way that learning should look.

- Teachers who leave after the bell aren't as hardworking as teachers who stay in the evening.

- If a leader goes in on weekends, they are much more invested in their school than those who don't work weekends at all.

- Students who are quiet in class are not learning at the same level as those students who raise their hands and are engaged.

- Lecture is harmful to student learning.

- Parents who live in poverty don't care about education as much as wealthier parents do.

- A colorful classroom is an engaging classroom.

"It's important to remember that it's not as much about what we like and don't like as it is about what practices are low value and what practices add value."

As an individual, partnership group, or team, what are some assumptions you would add to this list when it comes to schools, learning, and students? Write five of them below.

CLUTTER CHECK

1.

2.

3.

4.

5.

Anticipating Roadblocks

What is interesting here is that our assumptions can become a road-block to doing this work. In *Think Again*, Grant (2021) writes about the desirability bias, which is when "we allow our preferences to cloud our judgment" (p. 103). During this implementation and de-implementation work, we must make sure that our judgment is not clouded in such a way that we want to get rid of initiatives we don't like—that may actually work—and trade them in for other initiatives that may not work at all.

In the beginning of the book, I asked you to write down three of your beliefs about student learning and school and then add the relevant actions you take in support of those beliefs and the distractions you think prevent you from achieving them.

Please go back to that list of distractions. Again, an assumption is an idea or belief you possess without having any evidence to support it. I am going to ask you to question any possible assumptions as we end this section with a Clutter Check.

CLUTTER CHECK

In this Clutter Check, please write the distractions, and then on the following line, write the possible assumption you are making. Often what we perceive to be distractions may be helpful actions we just view as too challenging. Or those distractions may just need to be viewed through a different lens.

For example, faculty meetings are often seen as a distraction because people do not view them as helpful. Many faculty meetings are just a venue where a school leader shares information that could have been emailed. However, if that faculty meeting was flipped to center on a goal that focused on impacting student learning, perhaps the meeting would not be seen as a distraction. The power of the three beliefs activity is that when a group shares their beliefs, along with their relevant actions and distractions, the team can collaborate to look at those distractions through a new lens. Through discussion they can honestly share that faculty meetings are a distraction and brainstorm ways to improve that issue. This, of course, takes a team that strongly believes in psychological safety.

Now it's your turn. Write the distractions, and then think of any possible assumptions you may be making.

1. _____

Possible assumption:

2. _____

Possible assumption:

3. _____

Possible assumption:

Monitoring Our Minds—Mindset

Rhinesmith (1992) defines mindset as "a predisposition to see the world in a particular way . . . a filter through which we look at the world" (p. 63). At the beginning of this chapter, in the "Case in Point" section, I provided a personal story on how I had to change the way I presented content during a two-day workshop I was facilitating. Additionally, in the "Emotions Over Evidence" section, I wrote about several procedures that leaders and teachers value but that may need to be replaced with something more valuable. To do this work, we must be open to reducing or replacing something we have long valued.

TIPS TO CONSIDER

- Collect evidence of impact to see if those strategies you value are working.

- If you are feeling exhausted, trust the feeling. If you find that you run out of time because you overplanned, consider planning less and provide more time for students and teachers to process information.

- COVID-19 taught us how to shift from one minute to the next, but we are always at risk of reverting to old habits, especially when we consistently hear about COVID learning loss. Covering more and cramming information won't make up for a loss. Covering less and going deeper with it will.

In the End

If schools do not begin to set boundaries, those outside of schools never will. A good way to persuade decision-makers up and down (particularly up) the organizational line is with evidence. Therefore, it is important for us to understand that implementation should be an evidence-based process that makes us highly selective about what we bring into our schools. For us to dive deep into this process, we needed to look at implementation science and use a model that helps us be thoughtful about this work. The Practical, Robust Implementation and Sustainability Model (PRISM) I introduced can be an impactful tool. PRISM allows teams to consider possible blind spots in their process.

I want to highlight here the external environment focus. Sometimes the external environment may be the parents or the larger school community. Instructional leadership teams should not only consider these groups but also understand how to communicate to them any improvements the school may be engaged in. Family engagement, for example, is not optional in the work of creating schools where children succeed. Failure to pay attention to this could mean the undoing of a promising endeavor.

DISCUSSION QUESTIONS

1. How might the PRISM method be helpful for your team when it comes to implementation and de-implementation?

2. What aspect of PRISM was the most useful for you?

3. What are your thoughts on the research that focuses on organizations and publishers using brain images to persuade buyers that they are credible sources?

4. What are some challenges your team is concerned about when it comes to de-implementation?

The De-implementation Research

Research

(with practical adaptations)

2

Low value means research does not support it, student and staff voices are not being heard, ignoring the well-being of our students and staff.

—Anonymous

SUCCESS CRITERIA

By the end of this chapter, you will be able to define the following:

- What de-implementation means
- What low-value practices are
- Two types of de-implementation
- Formal and informal de-implementation
- Why it's necessary to engage in unlearning

Add two of your own success criteria:

-
-

Regardless of which country you are leading and teaching in, de-implementation isn't something you should just want to do as a school community; it is something your school community *needs* to do. Why? Because somewhere in all the hundreds of actions, activities, and initiatives you already engage in, along with those you want to engage in, there are countless ones you no longer need. Yet it's important to remember that engaging in new strategies is not an issue if they help provide an impact on student learning. That impact we are always looking for is at least a year's worth of growth for a year's input.

As someone who facilitates workshops and delivers keynotes, I know my job is to provide practical insight and strategies. For a while, though, I was uncomfortable that some people attended my workshops or keynotes with the hope of adopting yet another strategy, and I began to think de-implementation was about stopping them from having that mindset. I soon realized that my own assumptions about de-implementation were wrong, and that will be illustrated in the following Case in Point.

> "That impact we are always looking for is at least a year's worth of growth for a year's input."

CASE IN POINT

New Is Not Automatically Bad

Over the years I have been running workshops, I typically began each session with success criteria. I explained that I knew the presentation would be successful because I had learning intentions and success criteria tied to it. These criteria gave me the confidence that I would effectively lead learning for participants by the end of the presentation.

During summer 2021, I began asking the audience for their own success criteria. How would they know that they learned the content? There are always people in the audience who have no idea why they are there, because they were "voluntold" to be there, and I wanted to change that experience for them. However, after asking the audience for their success criteria, I noticed that most of the audience wanted to walk away with one new strategy. That's the popular answer, right? As educators, we go into every learning experience wanting to gain one more tool for our educational toolbox. However, de-implementation changed my mindset on that goal. I began telling the audience that should be the last thing they wanted to walk away with at the end of the presentation.

I suggested that the first action is to evaluate the strategies they are currently using to see if they are working. However, as my understanding of de-implementation evolved, I realized it's important to find new strategies. New strategies may help breathe new life into someone's career, or a new strategy could be the trick a teacher needs to elevate student voice in their classroom.

I realized I was assuming that de-implementation was merely about getting rid of practices that were not working, and I had not considered that de-implementation was also about bringing in new practices that could add value to the student learning experience.

I'd like to provide some food for thought: If discovering new ideas is not a bad thing, then maybe what teachers and leaders can do when attending workshops and keynotes is an activity to make sure they are leaving those venues with the best possible list of strategies for their classroom or school.

In the following Clutter Check, try this strategy to make sure you aren't adding too much to your plate.

The next time you attend a workshop, try this activity I learned from Jeana Williams and Melody Morgan from the Arkansas Public School Resource Center (APSRC). Take the following steps:

CLUTTER CHECK

- Grab a paper plate when you get home after the workshop.

- Write down all the strategies you picked up during the session that you promised yourself you would use back at school.

- Cross out three of the strategies you swore you would use.

- The ones left on the plate are probably the ones you can commit to.

Defining De-implementation

If teachers and leaders begin engaging in de-implementation, it will help foster deeper and more impactful practices. After all, leaders and teachers can't go deep if they're spread too thin. But note: de-implementation must be based in both direct and indirect evidence; so please do not close the book yet and say, "Woo-hoo! Let's start getting rid of stuff we don't like!" It is far more deliberate than that.

What I'm referring to here is conscious de-implementation. We need to make a conscious effort to look at our practices and understand whether they are impactful or not. If they are not, we need to understand why. It may be that we need to approach them differently or replace them with something that is far better for our students. Before we can embark on this journey, however, we need to know what de-implementation is.

> "We need to make a conscious effort to look at our practices and understand whether they are impactful or not."

The Science

De-implementation is based in the dissemination and implementation science shared in Chapter 1. Van Bodegom-Vos et al. (2017) define de-implementation as the process of "abandoning existing low-value practices." This research originated in the medical field, but recently studies have been published in the field of school psychology as well.

In fact, when looking at the research from a social-science perspective, which is quite a new concept, McKay et al. (2018, p. 190) define de-implementation "as the discontinuation of interventions that should no longer be provided." The key to the research, and what makes it so difficult to agree on at times, is the term "low-value practices" and the process behind deciding which interventions "should no longer be provided."

Before your team can begin the work of defining low-value practices, or those practices that should no longer be provided, it's important to consider your *why*. De-implementation shouldn't be seen as the shiny new toy; so this Clutter Check focuses on why you believe you need to move forward with this work in the first place.

CLUTTER CHECK

Please take a moment to define your *why*. Answer the following questions:

- Why are you interested in de-implementation?

- What do you hope the process of de-implementation will do for your classroom or school?

- What are your success criteria? Meaning, what does successful de-implementation look like for your classroom or school?

"Low-Value" Misconceptions

What I learned while researching this book is that what is considered low value to one person may in fact be high value to another. This tension does not necessarily happen because either party has a plethora of research on how effective the practice is but more because, as discussed in Chapter 1, one person likes the practice and the other does not.

McKay et al. (2018, p. 190) use an example of the Drug Abuse Resistance Education program (D.A.R.E.), which was implemented in many schools but was not supported by research. They write, "When evidence of effectiveness became part of the criteria for obtaining federal funding, the program was revised in 2003 but failed to demonstrate effectiveness" (p. 192). However, the researchers go on to say, "D.A.R.E. continues to be widely implemented; the program estimates that it is present in 75% of the nation's school districts and is taught in all 50 states" (p. 192). McKay et al. suggest that there are many interventions within the social-science field that have not been evidence-based but have been maintained "via persuasion, training, or tradition" (p. 190).

As a teacher in a high-poverty city school in 2002, I remember having the D.A.R.E. program in our school and loving the idea behind it, but I also remember that in the 2004 school year it was no longer offered because funding was cut due to lack of evidence that it worked. It felt right, but the bottom line is that it was wrong. Our feelings and instincts are powerful persuaders and can at times mislead us.

What also makes low value an interesting area of tension is that when I began surveying leaders and teachers in coaching sessions and workshops, I found that many people considered low-value practices the ones that they felt were done to them, as opposed to any practices they voluntarily engaged in within their classroom or school. Objectively, we know that something imposed externally can be an effective practice. But if there has been no buy-in or proper training, that effectiveness may never have the chance to reveal itself.

The Reality of "Low-Value" Practices

To provide some research, and a bit of a deeper understanding here, Farmer et al. (2021) suggest that low-value practices are those that

- have not been shown to be effective and efficacious,

- are less effective or efficacious than another available practice,

- cause harm, or

- are no longer necessary.

McKay et al. (2018) write, "Dissemination and implementation science, which is dedicated to enhancing the successful uptake and implementation of research, increasingly recognizes the importance of also understanding when and how it is appropriate to decrease or end interventions" (p. 189). It's important to understand the circumstances for when de-implementation is appropriate.

In fact, de-implementation should be seen as a way to build sustainability within schools. McKay et al. (2018, p. 190) narrow Farmer et al.'s (2021) work a bit to three circumstances or criteria for when de-implementation is appropriate:

> "In fact, de-implementation should be seen as a way to build sustainability within schools."

(a) **When interventions lack effectiveness or are harmful**— This means that educators must be aware of declining data; increases in negative data such as the number of students asked to leave their classroom to go to the main office or number of suspensions; or a decrease in student and/or staff engagement. All of these speak to low effectiveness or poor fidelity.

(b) **When more effective or efficient interventions become available**—This is an area where educators need to be careful, because they will want to ensure that the new practice is better than what they are already using and that they are not simply chasing after the next hot fad.

(c) **When the health or social issue of concern dissipates**—This research is from the medical field; so another way of looking at this within our educational context would be to say when the area of need is no longer there. Take a Multi-Tiered System of Support (MTSS), which offers targeted support for students who are struggling. At some point the interventions will work and the student will not need that targeted support any longer. This is difficult because sometimes MTSS and its counterparts, like Academic Intervention Services (AIS), are used as a gateway to identify a student for special education, as opposed to being seen as short-term targeted support to help students become successful.

CLUTTER CHECK

- What is a strength of starting a de-implementation process in your school?
- What is a weakness of beginning a de-implementation process?
- What is an opportunity that the de-implementation process may create for your school or district?
- What is a threat to the de-implementation process in your school or district?

Two Types of De-implementation

Wang et al. (2018) suggest that de-implementation comes down to four areas: partial reduction, complete reversal, substitution with related replacement, and substitution with unrelated replacement of existing practice. When we look at these four areas, it seems a bit complicated, right? I'd prefer to uncomplicate the topic and look at it as a process teachers and leaders go through to be more minimalist in their practice. Yes, perhaps when we work in the medical field it must be complicated due to compliance issues, but within education we can streamline a bit.

For our purposes I have consolidated the work of Wang et al. (2018) and suggest it might be more useful for educators to focus on two areas instead of four. What I am proposing is that we continue to use partial reduction but we take the other three and combine them into a category called replacement action (see Figure 2.1).

Figure 2.1

- Partial reduction
- Complete reversal
- Substitution with related replacement
- Substitution with unrelated replacement of existing practice

Partial reduction

Replacement action

Wang et al. (2018) offer us support in this suggestion: "Partial reduction/reversal of practice may require minimal learning effort because new skills are not required for an established practice, but some degree of education is needed on the new evidence" (p. 106). They go on to say, "Complete reversal or discontinuation of an existing practice without replacement may require significant effort to overcome confirmation bias or loss aversion that might slow or prevent discontinuation" (p. 106).

There is an additional reason why I am suggesting consolidating the four aspects of de-implementation into two aspects, and that is because regardless of what we discontinue, we will replace that time with something else—likely the opportunity to go deeper with another practice that is more worthwhile.

Before we move any further, I'll ask you to process this information in the Clutter Check. I want you to consider how you have done this work before. Although you may not know it, you have most likely already partially reduced or replaced an action in your teaching and leading.

"Regardless of what we discontinue, we will replace that time with something else—likely the opportunity to go deeper with another practice that is more worthwhile."

CLUTTER
CHECK

In your career as a teacher or leader, what have you partially reduced in your practices before? For example, have you ever partially reduced the amount of homework you gave to students each night? Write your example here: _____

_____

_____

In your career as a teacher or leader, think of a time when you engaged in a replacement action because something you were doing was not working. For example, you used to lecture a lot, then moved in the direction of engaging in cooperative learning for students instead. Write your example here: _____

_____

_____

Formal and Informal De-implementation

One of the other important considerations is that of informal and formal de-implementation. In Chapter 4, a formal de-implementation process is introduced for significant school change to make sure that decisions to reduce or replace are well thought out. However, the reality is that not every partial reduction or replacement action needs a formal process. If a teacher in the classroom realizes they are lecturing too much and decides in the moment to move to a collaborative learning model so students can process information, they are certainly not going to ask students to sit quietly while they fill out a de-implementation checklist. The anecdote about the two-day workshop I was facilitating, in the "Case in Point" section in Chapter 1, is a good example of an informal de-implementation. I was providing too many slides and too much information. I needed to quickly reduce that number and replace it with a more practical activity for the audience to engage in. That change improved the learning in a matter of minutes.

In addition, if teachers and leaders are going to have fewer meetings or check email less often, they do not need to engage in a formal process to do that work. An informal process of de-implementation represents those practices that can be done quickly because we realize they are just not providing the impact we need. What does remain constant in either process is the need to make sure that the decision is based in evidence. Research from reputable sources is one form of data, but if you are constantly exhausted or frustrated, that is a form of data too.

The formal de-implementation process needs to be initiated when leadership teams, professional learning communities, or departments are going to change their grading policies, change their literacy program, or do anything else that will impact a large group of teachers and students. The formal de-implementation process is for those initiatives and activities that may impact an entire school community.

Cues for Formal or Informal De-implementation

TYPE	GUIDING STATEMENTS	EXAMPLES
Informal de-implementation	I can make this change on my own. It impacts only me or my immediate team. I can begin this change immediately. I can see change within a day.	Checking email Short response times for students during class discussions Frequency of late nights
Formal de-implementation	This change requires a team. This change impacts most of the school. This change requires data collection from a variety of sources. It could take many months or a year to see a result.	Shifting the middle school science program Student discipline procedures Levels of family engagement

Anticipating Roadblocks

It's important to understand that there are positive reasons for focusing on de-implementation, but negative issues will arise as well. For example, during a keynote focusing on instructional leadership, I brought up the topic of de-implementation, and the assistant superintendent who had brought me in to provide the keynote was heavily concerned people within his district would just stop doing things they didn't like. Therefore, a weakness of de-implementation is that if it is not done correctly, it might cause a bit of lawlessness, and we do not want that. Therefore, I have included a de-implementation checklist in this book, which can be found in Chapter 4. That is also why I offer an intermission section in the book where I focus on the difference between formal and informal de-implementation. If you are concerned that colleagues will go about de-implementation in the wrong way, consider doing the following:

- Using your instructional leadership team for the formal de-implementation process in your school

- Clearly articulating at staff meetings how to de-implement

- Sending staff a blog or article on de-implementation as a precursor to a meeting or as a follow-up after a staff meeting

And keep in mind:

- Teachers and leaders will value de-implementation if superintendents and district offices value de-implementation.

- People who feel safe will be more likely to engage in open discussions about what works and what doesn't.

- When people complain about initiative fatigue, we should probably listen.

Monitoring Our Minds: Unlearning and Relearning

One area that makes de-implementation challenging at times is that it will involve unlearning and relearning on the part of the educators engaged in the process. We have all been so trained to follow the rules and engage in compliance. We are conditioned as educators to take on more and more for the good of the students, when it may not be good for the students at all.

Wang et al. (2018) suggest, "Unlearning is a process of discarding outdated mental models to make room for alternative models" (p. 106). Dutta (2019) writes that "relearning efforts are grounded in gaining and embodying new knowledge" (p. 3).

For example, when COVID-19 came crashing into our lives, teachers, students, parents, and leaders were asked to go from in-person teaching and learning to pandemic teaching and learning. We were forced to unlearn how we normally operated and relearn new ways to do everything. We had to change our idea of what teaching and learning looked like and figure out how to engage students who were no longer in front of us in a classroom. De-implementation takes unlearning and relearning to help deconstruct our old mental models of how we should operate. You can go about unlearning and relearning in a few ways.

In the End

Conscious de-implementation is important because when we do it, we are taking back the power in our classrooms, schools, and districts. We are exerting our control over the initiatives and actions we are often confined by, taking positive steps toward managing our time differently, and focusing on doing less to have more of an impact on student learning.

TIPS TO UNLEARN AND RELEARN

- Instead of entering professional learning hoping for a new strategy, begin thinking about how the content being learned fits into your present situation, and whether you are implementing the practice correctly.

- Make a list of any activities, within your own practices, you currently partake in. Then push yourself to find objective evidence that each one is effective. This will take some brutal, internal honesty.

- Notice when you have a strong reaction to an idea, particularly a negative emotion. Explore that discomfort to try to get at its roots.

- If you are exploring this work as a partner or part of a team, consider how you presently engage in discussions, if at all, and consider how you may need to unlearn the roles around the table. (In my collective leader efficacy work, I ask teams to assign roles to everyone around the table, consider the role of status in how they function, and use protocols to focus on intentional professional learning at each meeting.)

As you read, de-implementation must be based on research and evidence. As Farmer et al. (2021) suggest, low-value practices are those practices that

- have not been shown to be effective and efficacious,

- are less effective or efficacious than another available practice,

- cause harm, or

- are no longer necessary.

This chapter also defined two ways to de-implement:

1) Partial reduction—do less of a practice that is already in place.

2) Replacement action—remove a practice and replace it with something better (including more time to focus on current practices that are effective).

As we move on, keep these three points in mind: First, we must understand which strategies are working and which ones are not. Second, we know that workload is at an all-time high, and high workload takes teachers and leaders away from their most important work, which is to focus on student learning. Last, this is a mental health issue. Too often, leaders and teachers talk about well-being but do very little about it. De-implementation should be considered as a strategy to begin finding well-being within our positions as teachers and leaders.

The next chapter will go deeper into the criteria for what to de-implement, with many relevant examples. It will also set the foundation for how to begin a formal de-implementation with your team.

DISCUSSION QUESTIONS

1. How would you define de-implementation?

2. McKay et al. (2018) and Farmer et al. (2021) suggest there are criteria for identifying what needs to be de-implemented. How will you use that information as you begin to engage in the de-implementation process?

3. What are your initial thoughts about what needs to be de-implemented in your classroom or school?

4. What do you see as the biggest barriers to engaging in this work?

INTERMISSION

Beliefs, Distractions, and Opportunities for Change

I'm a fan of the arts, especially stage shows. During most Broadway and West End shows or off-Broadway and off–West End shows, there is an intermission. It gives us time to run to the restroom—and hope there isn't a line—and perhaps grab our favorite beverage. During that time, we reflect on what we just saw and think about what may be coming next in the performance.

My hope is that this topic of de-implementation is part drama and part comedy. The comedy should be the fun you have while engaging in this process. Take time during your conversations to laugh with one another. Learning should be joyful. We need more comedy in our lives! For the intermission in this book, there is one activity and one clarification.

At the beginning of the book, I asked you to write three beliefs using the image you see below. On the left side, you wrote the relevant activities you engage in to support those beliefs. On the right side, you wrote the actions that distract you from obtaining those beliefs.

Let's use the following activity to see if any of that information has changed. Once again, write your three beliefs, as well as relevant actions and distractions. Take time to notice if any of them have changed.

Additionally, I have added an image to help you brainstorm your ideas focusing on distractions. Here I'll ask to you write down the distractions to see if there is anything you can do differently. For example, people will talk about faculty meetings being a distraction because they are agenda-driven and not helpful. However, through conversations as a team when it comes to de-implementation, people share their concerns about the ineffectiveness of faculty meetings, and the team may move forward toward a flipped faculty meeting process.

DISTRACTING

3 Beliefs

1.

2.

3.

RELEVANT

WHAT I CAN DO INSTEAD

DISTRACTION

Now take a moment to process the information from Chapters 1 and 2. I have included questions to help you:

How are implementation and de-implementation interrelated?

How do our assumptions factor into both implementation and de-implementation?

When it comes to the three beliefs you wrote down in the beginning of the book, how might de-implementation help you?

I thought de-implementation was about . . .

One area of de-implementation I did not consider is . . .

One thing I wonder when it comes to de-implementation is . . .

What Gets De-implemented

3

(based on reflection and evidence)

To be honest, I think I have partially reduced all that I can as an administrator.

—Anonymous

SUCCESS CRITERIA

By the end of this chapter, you will be able to identify the following:

- Initiatives that fit partial reduction or replacement action

- Examples of evidence to collect to understand impact

- The criteria for the de-implementation process

- Questions to guide the de-implementation process

- Examples of where your classroom or school could de-implement

Write two success criteria of your own:

-

-

The opening quotation resonated with me when I first read it among the survey results of what educators would consider de-implementing. We often feel as though there is nothing we can do to minimize the workload we face day in and day out; however, that is not true. One of the reasons I had you write your three beliefs at the beginning of the book—and revisit them, along with the relevant actions and distractions—is that this simple process can help you see some of the other activities and initiatives on your plate that you may be able to reduce or replace.

Through dialogue and understanding of de-implementation, and the criteria behind it, we can begin finding areas that no longer need our attention. In fact, I would suggest that it's educational malpractice not to look at what we can begin de-implementing.

It's early in this chapter, but I would like you to engage in a Clutter Check. Just as with the opening quotation, there are times when we believe we have exhausted all efforts only to find that within some of our

CASE IN POINT

A Look in the Mirror

A few years ago, I was working with a principal in Canada who was very frustrated by the number of initiatives their school division was focusing on. The division lacked direction, and it was something the principal desperately wanted to work on. They often spoke about how annoying it was that the division was forcing principals to focus on all these different initiatives at the same time yet gathering little evidence to see if they were working.

Interestingly, when it was their turn to lead meetings, each meeting focused on a different instructional strategy. In October it was reciprocal teaching, in November the jigsaw method, and in December questioning techniques. The following January, when I sat down to work with the principal, they once again began complaining about division initiatives. I asked questions about the principal's own meetings, and they proudly spoke to the different strategies they were focused on. When I followed up with a question about evidence of impact, the principal could not provide any.

The principal realized they were doing the same thing to their teachers that they thought the division was doing to them. The only difference was that the principal felt they had control over the initiatives and genuinely believed they were helping the teachers. I mentioned that the directors at the division level probably felt the same.

Instead of focusing on a new instructional strategy at each meeting, we discussed how the principal could flip their meetings and send out a short article highlighting a strategy, then at the faculty meeting discuss the pros and cons of using it or model it and let the teachers practice in the moment. Furthermore, I suggested they could discuss the success criteria of the strategy so all staff would have a common understanding of what success looks like, then give teachers the next month to try the strategy in their classroom and bring back evidence of its effectiveness.

Instead of hammering teachers with a new strategy every month, the principal slowed down the process by focusing on one strategy over a two-month period. This allowed them to deepen their learning as a staff and lessen the likelihood of initiative fatigue.

Take a little time to think about some favorite activities you engage in as a building leader, district leader, or teacher. Choose one activity and reflect on how it connects with your three beliefs. If it doesn't, perhaps you should tweak the activity. If it does, take time to consider how you know the activity is impacting students.

CLUTTER CHECK

_____

_____

_____

_____

favorite activities there is space to reduce or replace, because those activities, as much as we may like them, are not impactful in their present state.

Partial Reduction

A partial reduction is exactly what it sounds like. It provides us with the opportunity to partially reduce a practice we engage in. I believe this is where most people will start because it gives them the opportunity to dip their toes in the water of de-implementation. What we know is that all people form habits, so just like cutting back on fatty foods or drinking fewer glasses of wine each night, a partial reduction is one where we still get the stimulus but we begin weaning our neurons off it and moving in a different direction.

Partial reduction provides the opportunity to treat practices differently when we engage with them more intentionally. It also allows us the chance to spend the time we get back engaging in other actions, such as getting into classrooms to build relationships, providing feedback to students in more authentic ways, or going home at a reasonable time to be with our families. (See Figure 3.1 for examples of partial reduction.)

Figure 3.1

EXAMPLES OF PARTIAL REDUCTION	
INITIATIVE	WHY REDUCE IT?
Meetings	Educators indicate that they attend too many meetings. As we know, meetings overlap and we often focus on the same topic at numerous meetings, which is not always the best use of our time.
District administration content	Too often, building leaders attend K–12 admin meetings where they are delivered content they do not have time to process. K–12 administration can surely provide content, but they must partially reduce it to allow the building leaders processing time.
Email	Educators and school leaders indicated that they spend too much time checking email or waiting for the next email to come into their inbox. Email controls their actions, so these educators and leaders are committing to checking email only three times a day and not letting email bleed into their family time at home.
Assessments	We have a habit of overassessing students and not doing anything with the assessments because we run out of time. Assessments serve little purpose if they are not used to drive instruction. We can also get just as much information using other methods of instruction.
Teacher talk versus student talk	On average, adults spend a great deal of time talking in the classroom. Educators are trying to decrease their amount of talking and increase student dialogue.
Homework	There are countless studies that speak to the ineffectiveness of homework. Alfie Kohn wrote *The Homework Myth* in 2006, and it set off a chain reaction for teachers looking at the amount of homework they were giving students.

What does homework look like in your school? Are there teachers who are light on homework, some who give large amounts, and others who are somewhere in the middle? Perhaps it's time to look at homework from a formal de-implementation role where the school community reduces homework to maximize impact on student learning. After all, just because students do more homework doesn't mean they are more prepared for learning.

Keys to effective homework:

- Small amounts that are relevant to the learning students are engaged in within their classroom

- More cohesive understanding among all teachers, especially at the middle school and high school level, so students do not get overwhelmed with homework

- Teachers ensuring that if they are going to assign homework, they have time to provide feedback on it

CLUTTER CHECK

Replacement Actions

Replacement actions apply to those areas that need to be replaced because they are ineffective overall. For example, we cannot partially reduce low expectations of students in special education, zero tolerance policies, or the practice of separating students by gender.

There is another way to look at replacement actions, from a more personal standpoint. I am a daily practitioner of meditation. I began meditation practices about four years ago when I was feeling an increase in stress, anxiety, and a realization that my ego was taking over my work and life. I began meditating for about five minutes in the morning, which meant that I stopped checking email or social media for five minutes so I could breathe, relax, and focus. Yes, it was a lot to ask of five minutes!

Over the years, my practice has evolved into fifteen to twenty minutes in the morning and again in the evening. What this means is that I intentionally replaced time I was spending on social media with time in my space where I could breathe and focus. The benefit is that the focus I have strengthened during the practice has spread into my conversations at home and in workshops or coaching and has also helped me rethink my actions before I engage in them.

"Replacement action is not just about replacing one action with another. Rather, it is about replacing a dysfunctional action with one that is more intentional and productive."

You do not have to practice meditation, although I think we all could use some time to slow down. My point is that a replacement action is not just about replacing one action with another. Rather, it is about replacing a dysfunctional action with one that is more intentional and productive.

In Figure 3.2 below, you will see some examples of strategies, mindsets, and policies educators are focusing on when it comes to replacement actions.

Figure 3.2

EXAMPLES OF REPLACEMENT ACTIONS		
INITIATIVE	WHY REPLACE IT?	WHAT THEY DO INSTEAD
Zero tolerance policies	Over the past few years, many schools have begun to eradicate zero tolerance policies because those policies have been shown to be discriminatory toward marginalized populations. In addition, zero tolerance policies have not been, by their very name, open to interpretation when it comes to how students are disciplined.	Schools are beginning to look at equitable discipline practices such as Positive Behavioral Interventions and Supports (PBIS), restorative justice, or proactive approaches to engaging students through a positive school climate to stop issues before they start.
Off-campus professional development to site-based professional development	Robinson and Timperley (2007) found that five leadership dimensions are critical in fostering impactful learning in a school community: "providing educational direction; ensuring strategic alignment; creating a community that learns how to improve student success; engaging in constructive problem talk; and selecting and developing smart tools" (p. 247).	Many schools are turning to site-based professional development, which is focused on a cycle of inquiry approach to learning. Le Fevre et al. (2019) suggest that there are six roots to facilitating impactful professional learning: "adopting an evaluative inquiry stance; valuing and using deep conceptual knowledge; being agentic; being aware of cultural positioning; being metacognitive; and bringing in a systemic focus" (pp. 7–8).

| Low expectations of special education students | Unfortunately, students classified as special education sometimes feel that their general education teachers have low expectations of them due to their classification. In fact, Butrymowicz and Mader (2017) found, "Special education students across the country reported low expectations in school, regardless of their actual ability level or future plans." | General education teachers and special education teachers are involved in co-planning for lessons and co-grading when it comes to all the students within their classrooms. Co-planning helps general education teachers elevate expectations and helps both parties develop engagement strategies that are good for all students. |

The Foundations of Your De-implementation Plan

When considering de-implementation, instructional leadership teams should focus on what they can partially reduce or what needs to be replaced. The examples above were meant to stimulate your thinking on what you feel could and should be de-implemented in your setting. Now the book will turn to a more in-depth understanding of the criteria for what gets replaced, gathering evidence, and using guiding questions to drive the overall de-implementation process. This will lay a solid foundation as you prepare to formally de-implement some practices in your school.

Criteria for What Gets De-Implemented

Remember, according to McKay et al. (2018) in Chapter 2, there are four criteria for what gets de-implemented:

- **The program/practice being de-implemented has not been shown to be effective and impactful.** Think . . .
  - Popcorn reading
  - Frequent PowerPoint lessons
  - Preparing notes for students (rather than their taking notes themselves)
  - Excessive lecturing

- **The program/practice being de-implemented is less effective or impactful than another available.** Think . . .
  - One-size-fits-all professional development
  - Spending most of the time at your desk (office or classroom)
  - Homework

- **The program/practice being de-implemented causes harm.** Think . . .
  - Zero tolerance policies
  - Fixed grouping (as opposed to flexible)
  - K–2 with little phonics instruction

- **The program/practice being de-implemented is no longer necessary.** Think . . .
  - Chalkboards
  - Study hall
  - Five-pound textbooks

While some practices are relatively easy to fit into certain categories, the crux of this work is relying on evidence. The question then becomes: How do we know whether the initiative is effective or not? How do we know whether the initiative has caused harm? We need to gather evidence to understand the impact of the initiatives.

"The question then becomes: How do we know whether the initiative is effective or not?"

Gathering Evidence

Evidence is an important consideration for the work your team is trying to do. We all need evidence, whether we are looking into how instructional strategies work in the classroom or trying to understand our own spirituality. How many of you have asked for a sign from God or the universe to help you understand why you're going through a certain situation?

Evidence helps us quantify our actions, but that quantifiable evidence usually comes in two forms: direct evidence and indirect evidence.

Direct Evidence

Direct evidence may come heavily from quantitative studies. For example, when evaluating literacy programs, it is always a good idea to look to research and get an understanding of how a program has impacted phonemic awareness, phonics, vocabulary, fluency, and comprehension. This means someone, or a group of people, from your instructional leadership team will have to gather the research behind the initiative.

The other way to consider direct evidence is to examine the impact it has on actual students in your school. According to DePaul University Teaching Commons (2022), "Direct evidence of student learning is tangible, visible, and measurable and tends to be more compelling evidence of exactly what students have and have not learned." For example, if a school is looking to replace their zero tolerance policy with a more equitable or proactive way to help students with their behavior, they can look at their discipline rates. This means they look at the number of students who are sent to the office with a referral or the number who are suspended from school. School officials can even gather direct evidence when it comes to the gender or race of those students who are being disciplined the most. One thing to keep in mind here is that the evidence gathered should be measured against a reliable standard. I often look to the National Center for Education Statistics for comparisons.

Indirect Evidence

When it comes to indirect evidence, DePaul University Teaching Commons (2022) suggests that it "tends to be composed of proxy signs that students are probably learning." Think of this as the more qualitative side of evidence. Qualitative studies can be very helpful in shaping our thinking and understanding. For example, schools are taking time to understand student perspectives through empathy interviews and student voice groups. In these conversations with students, students provide their perspective on teaching and learning to teachers and leaders.

Examples of Evidence-Based Decisions

In Figure 3.3 below, I have included examples of initiatives to be de-implemented as well as columns for direct evidence and indirect evidence. For uniformity's sake, I am going to use some of the same examples I provided earlier. Additionally, you will notice that in most of these cases, direct evidence is that of research studies. It's important to note that in my collective leader efficacy work, when referring to different roles that members of the instructional leadership can take, researcher is a key role I have suggested. It is highly important when considering de-implementation that we use research to help us understand which programs have been found to be effective. I will explore this on a deeper level in the next chapter.

"It is highly important when considering de-implementation that we use research to help us understand which programs have been found to be effective."

Figure 3.3

CRITERIA FOR DE-IMPLEMENTATION			
CRITERIA	DE-IMPLEMENTATION EXAMPLE	DIRECT EVIDENCE	INDIRECT EVIDENCE
The program being de-implemented has not been shown to be effective and impactful.	D.A.R.E.	Research studies, student discipline rates	Student feedback about D.A.R.E. program through exit interviews
The program being de-implemented is less effective or impactful than another available.	Reading Recovery	Research studies, Lexile levels, phonemic awareness levels, and the like	Desire of students to read independently
The program being de-implemented causes harm.	Zero tolerance policies	Research studies, student discipline data disaggregated by race	Student surveys or empathy interviews by students
The program being de-implemented is no longer necessary.	Study halls being replaced with a more focused independent study	Research/student assessment data	Focus groups of adults and students

I understand that I wrote "research studies" as direct evidence for each of the examples, which was intentional. One of the areas of intentionality I would like your team to take away from this is that whenever your school team considers a new program or initiative, your go-to action should be to look at research studies to see the benefits or the negative aspects of that program or initiative. Below I have provided some examples of high-quality sources to gather evidence (see Figure 3.4).

Figure 3.4

Gold-Standard Resources for Gathering Evidence

Education Week—The Education Week Research Center is publishing impactful research that is both current and timely.

Australian Council for Educational Leaders (ACEL)—ACEL is a leadership organization that offers deep research and practical guidance, which will help elevate the impact of any building or district leader.

Learning Forward—Whether for its literature focusing on research and practice or its professional learning opportunities, Learning Forward is among the most important educational learning organizations.

New Pedagogies for Deep Learning (NPDL)—Michael Fullan is the global director of this organization. NPDL houses research-based articles, webinars, and professional learning opportunities.

International Congress for School Effectiveness and Improvement (ICSEI)—ICSEI is an international organization that offers research-based articles and studies, as well as in-person and online professional learning.

ASCD's Educational Leadership—This has always been one of my favorite journals because of the research and practice they publish every month.

SAGE Journals—Whether you are looking for research-based articles, doctoral dissertations, or studies, this is the largest database of educational research in the world.

Meta^X—John Hattie's visible learning research is housed under the title Meta^X. It is not just the influences and their effect sizes; Meta^X includes the research Hattie has used in developing his meta-meta-analysis.

Tom Guskey—If a person can supply a gold standard in research, then Guskey is that person for me. Anything he writes is supported by research, much of which he has done himself, and is extremely relevant.

Guiding Questions

Last, developing success criteria will be important for de-implementation. After all, your team needs to define in advance how they will know the de-implementation process is successful. Do the people experiencing the de-implementation see an improvement in other areas after they de-implement? For example, a principal from Arkansas whom I work with as part of a partnership with Arkansas State University and EDUTAS contacted me to say he began partially reducing his use of email and, after a few weeks setting boundaries, found that he had more time to get into classrooms. He also found that he spent less time in his office and more time engaging in conversations with students and teachers. He continues to see improvement. Although he did not need to engage in a formal process to figure it out, his partial reduction bought him time in other areas.

How do we develop questions to help us guide de-implementation? This is where we can return to Tom Guskey's six questions, shared in Chapter 1. After careful consideration, I believe they are equally

Figure 3.5

QUESTIONS	DE-IMPLEMENTATION
What are the specific goals of the program?	What are the specific goals for de-implementing this initiative? What will you gain in other areas if you de-implement this area?
How valuable or important are those goals?	Are those goals worth de-implementing this initiative in your school or classroom?
What evidence would you trust to verify those goals were met?	What evidence will you collect to understand successful de-implementation?
Would all stakeholders in the program trust the same evidence?	During the success criteria development, when engaging in de-implementation, co-create a list of possible evidence.
How soon would you expect to attain that evidence?	What type of timeline will your team set to understand successful de-implementation?
How much "improvement" is sufficient (cost-effectiveness)?	How does this de-implementation lead to improvement? Has it been cost-effective?

important for identifying which programs should be de-implemented. Those questions, along with my explanations, are in Figure 3.5.

Questions help guide our practices. They give us a framework for thinking, which is why teachers and workshop facilitators use open-ended questions all the time. These questions help take us to a deeper level of learning. There is another important aspect to these questions and the role of de-implementation in our lives: that the questions and de-implementation can help us understand our locus of control as well as how to react when confronted with issues that come from outside our locus of control. More on this in the "Monitoring Our Minds" section.

Anticipating Roadblocks

Too often when I am presenting on the topic of de-implementation and ask where leaders and teachers would start this work, I am confronted by examples that those in the workshop do not control. For example, a very popular answer is to de-implement the school improvement process. I usually address this example in a couple of different ways. One way is to ask if there is any space for the improvement process to be improved (yes, I see the irony there!). The other way is to ask if there is room for clarity about what the process involves and whether people have creative space in how they comply with it.

To have the right focus on de-implementation, consider the following:

- When beginning the process of de-implementation, look first to those strategies or initiatives you control.

- Have discussions with your team about their locus of control, and define ways each member of the team has control over de-implementing strategies and initiatives.

Monitoring Our Minds: Locus of Control

In an article titled "The Past and Future of Teacher Efficacy," Guskey (2021) writes about attribution theory, which "describes the degree to which people believe they can affect and are responsible for different aspects of their lives." This was referred to as locus of control, which was developed by Julien Rotter. Guskey goes on to explain the following:

> Individuals with internal locus of control believe in their personal ability to direct themselves and influence situations.

They tend to be highly motivated and success oriented. People with external locus of control, by contrast, believe that what happens around them and the actions of others are things they cannot influence.

This explanation by Guskey is important because he goes on to explain that people with external locus of control have the perspective that

events in their life are determined by forces over which they have little control, or are due to chance or luck. They generally see things as happening to them and tend to be more passive and accepting.

The bottom line is this: If you as an educator or school leader view all your programs and initiatives through a lens of external locus of control, it will be very difficult to engage in de-implementation because you will always feel you don't have the authority to do it. In contrast, thinking about how we can change will unlock our ability to think outside the box. In doing so, we may find we have more control than we originally believed. We can stay focused and forge our way to professional and personal lives that are more fulfilling.

In the End

De-implementation is not cut-and-dried. I say that because we often approach these issues with a confirmation bias. I want to get rid of zero tolerance policies, so I'm going to look for research that says zero tolerance policies are destructive. But in doing the research behind zero tolerance policies, you will find they began as a way to keep students safe but turned into something more destructive in schools. There is a cautionary tale there for your team, because you must understand that most programs did not start from a negative place; our implementation or weak data may have contributed to their poor outcomes.

I reshared Tom Guskey's questions regarding program evaluation, using a de-implementation lens, because they are very helpful for instructional leadership teams. They provide a framework for teams to use as they consider de-implementation (and implementation). Intersecting Guskey's questions with McKay et al.'s criteria can help us greatly when engaging in de-implementation.

As we move forward to Chapter 4, we will focus on the formal de-implementation process.

DISCUSSION QUESTIONS

1. How might Tom Guskey's questions help your team in future conversations?

2. How often does your team discuss direct evidence and indirect evidence? How might this process help you as you move forward in the de-implementation process?

3. McKay et al. offer four criteria for the de-implementation process. What initiatives come to mind when considering each of those four criteria?

4. What evidence would you consider to change your mind about an initiative you are convinced needs to be de-implemented?

INTERMISSION

Top Ten List

It's time for you to brainstorm what your team wants to de-implement. You see, something led you to this book and this topic. In the next chapter, your team will learn about the cycle of de-implementation, but what I know to be true is that many ideas about what needs to be de-implemented are swirling around the team.

So in the section below, I want you to create your top ten list. What have you heard from staff when it comes to things they formally want off their plate? Not the small stuff; I'm talking the big fish, like grading, homework, discipline, and the like. To do that:

- Talk about de-implementation at the staff meeting.

- Do walk-throughs and learning walks focusing on student engagement, and see what's missing from classrooms . . . or what there is too much of.

- Do empathy interviews with students about what they would get rid of or add to their learning.

Now it's time for that top ten list that I know you or your team have in mind. Write the small and the big, but just know, the small usually does not need a formal process. The big stuff does!

1.

2.

3.

4.

5.

6.

7.

8.

9.

10.

Now cross out three that you feel you cannot commit to.

By the time you get to the last chapter, I want you to have narrowed your list down to one.

The Cycle of De-implementation

(for big ideas around school change)

4

I would like to replace graduation requirements to have more flexibility for students. Instead of specific courses (example through physical science-biology-chemistry as a required sequence), students would have the flexibility to take courses related to actual interests or careers. For example, horticulture or agriculture science could count as graduation requirements.

—Anonymous

SUCCESS CRITERIA

By the end of this chapter, you will be able to identify the following:

- The purpose and knowledge of using a cycle of de-implementation to do this work

- How to use a de-implementation checklist to do your best thinking around this work

- How to use a program logic model to help plan actionable steps

- Criteria for future collaborative work

Write two of your own success criteria:

-

-

With most things in life, a little practice is needed before you get your stride. Even ideas that seem straightforward on paper or in presentations can get a little clumsy when you take them into your own hands. Knowing this well as an educator, I dedicate this chapter to practice—specifically, practicing a model for formal de-implementation. While you, and hopefully your team, have ideas of what could be de-implemented in your school, you will now have the opportunity to go through a process step by step, increasing the chances of successful execution on the ground. This process is needed only when you are looking to remove a schoolwide practice and particularly if you want to replace it with something better. The example I use for this chapter demonstrates both removing and replacing with a new initiative to provide the most comprehensive use of the cycle.

First, let's return to your top ten list from the intermission on pages 59–60, which became a top seven list. Take one of the seven and use it as a test run for the de-implementation process. It may be tempting to skip some of the steps, but I caution against that. If the cycle of de-implementation is done correctly, it opens opportunities to do this process instinctively and with automaticity in other spaces. This can transform the efficiency of a school, building a culture of confidence and respect in the decisions that are made for the community.

To accomplish this, the next Case in Point focuses on a school that had a sneaking suspicion that their goal of student voice needed a replacement action. If you don't have a practice topic from your list, feel free to use this scenario to practice with the de-implementation cycle outlined in this chapter.

> "If the cycle of de-implementation is done correctly, it opens opportunities to do this process instinctively and with automaticity in other spaces."

CASE IN POINT

Reimagining Student Council

I was recently working with a high school leadership team. They were looking for ways to develop student voice because, although they included students in decision-making in a variety of ways, they thought it felt like window dressing. What they realized was that they spoke about the importance of student voice but often looked to the same students to provide that voice. Too many students still seemed to feel, and act, disenfranchised.

One of the areas we looked to was their student council. In the five years the leadership team had been together, the student council had seemed to be running in a silo and rarely had an impact on the decisions the school leadership team made. The principal, one of the assistant principals, the school psychologist, or the instructional coach on the team would attend student council meetings with the teacher-designated council chair, but they all felt as though they were just going through the motions. And sadly, most of the students on the student council didn't know any better, because they were engaged in planning activities that student councils always do.

After a deep discussion about de-implementation and differentiating between partial reductions or replacement actions, the leadership decided they wanted to replace the typical function of the student council. The leadership team and student council took to social media to gather information about alternative student council structures.

Both the adults from the school leadership team and the students on the council came back together to brainstorm ways to make sure the student council fostered the diverse voices that were already there and to look for other ways they could partner together. In this new partnership, they discussed how to give students more of a voice in their learning, such as with critical issues happening in society. They wanted to advance from a culture that said it valued diversity, equity, and student voice to a culture that modeled what that looked like.

It was hard work, and courageous, uncomfortable conversations needed to be had, but they found that engaging in those conversations was so much more impactful than the old ways of doing things.

The Cycle of De-implementation

One of the ways the above team came to the decision about student voice was through engaging in a cycle of inquiry, which for our purposes in this book, I am calling a cycle of de-implementation.

I have used cycles of inquiry for quite some time, in individual coaching, instructional teamwork, whole faculty focuses, and even in the state work I do. The cycle of de-implementation is that same type of process but streamlined to fit this work.

THE RESEARCH

Although the concept of cycle of inquiry can be dated back to Dewey (1911), Casey (2014) has produced some of the finest research on the topic of inquiry cycles. In fact, Casey writes, "The Inquiry Cycle describes learning in terms of a continuous dynamic of ask, investigate, create, discuss and reflect. Of these elements 'ask' has a privileged place. Questions are the root of inquiry; they initiate, sustain and invigorate each aspect of the process. Questions direct investigation, drive creativity, stimulate discussion and are the bedrock of reflection" (p. 510).

Casey (2014) goes on to write, "When we describe learning in terms of inquiry, we are clearly affirming that learning and questioning processes are somehow intertwined" (p. 510). We should always question our practices, because it may lead to less need for de-implementation in the future.

The very process of working with a team on de-implementation is a form of professional learning and development. As I wrote at the beginning of the book, Le Fevre et al. (2019) suggest that there are six roots to facilitating impactful professional learning: "adopting an evaluative inquiry stance; valuing and using deep conceptual knowledge; being agentic; being aware of cultural positioning; being metacognitive; and bringing in a systemic focus" (pp. 7–8).

The following is an inquiry stance that will allow for deep conceptual knowledge that is meant to develop agency among your team. Cultural positioning enters the process when taking time to understand the perspective and characteristics of your students and teachers. It will require you to think metacognitively. Regardless of where you start this process within your school community, it should add to your systemic focus of improving the quality of learning for students and teachers.

In Figure 4.1 (see page 66), I have included the cycle of de-implementation. Immediately following, I will demonstrate how it can be used for the de-implementation process. For our purposes in this section, I will model with transitioning from traditional grading to standards-based grading. Once you see my model, you can try it out with the scenario presented in the Case in Point or your own idea. I have provided some information below about traditional grading for context.

TRADITIONAL GRADING

These excerpts were pulled from a *Los Angeles Times* article headlined "Faced With Soaring Ds and Fs, Schools Are Ditching the Old Way of Grading." It perfectly captures the concerns about traditional grading. The author, Paloma Esquivel (2021), writes, "Educators are moving away from traditional point-driven grading systems, aiming to close large academic gaps among racial, ethnic and economic groups." Esquivel goes on to say,

> Los Angeles and San Diego Unified—the state's two largest school districts, with some 660,000 students combined—have recently directed teachers to base academic grades on whether students have learned what was expected of them during a course—and not penalize them for behavior, work habits and missed deadlines.

Finally, Esquivel reports, "Traditional grading has often been used to 'justify and to provide unequal educational opportunities based on a student's race or class,' said a letter sent by Yoshimoto-Towery and Pedro A. Garcia, senior executive director of the division of instruction, to principals last month."

Key Elements

Each part of the cycle will have supporting tools and templates. See page 66 for a snapshot of these in Figure 4.2. As we get into the process, you will explore them in detail.

Step 1: Inquire

Step 1 is where we inquire into what needs to be de-implemented. In this part of the cycle, the focus is on internal inquiry for the instructional team. It is where they set aside time to engage in authentic discussions that help them clearly articulate why an initiative is under review and what will be needed to get started. It has two sections. The first section is divided into three parts: **developing a purpose statement, defining an inquiry question, and creating a theory of action**. The second section shifts to considering the evidence your team needs to gather.

Figure 4.1

Cycle of De-implementation

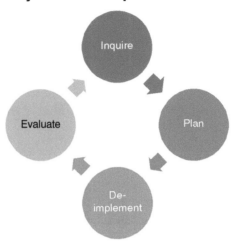

Figure 4.2

KEY ELEMENTS FOR THE CYCLE OF DE-IMPLEMENTATION	
Inquire	• Purpose statement
	• Inquiry questions
	• Theory of action
	• Evidence collection
Plan	• Program logic model
De-implement	• The de-implementation checklist
	• Action steps list
Evaluate	• Evaluation tool

Purpose Statement

The purpose statement is where you define the motivation behind the inquiry. Again, I return to the example of a school district replacing its traditional report card with a standards-based report card.

MY MODEL

Guiding question—How do we engage in more equitable grading practices?

Sample problem framed—Historically, our school has used traditional letter grading that has not been uniform, which means students in our school do not benefit from equitable grading practices. We are considering de-implementing traditional grading practices because we want our grading to be more equitable.

Purpose statement—The purpose of this inquiry is to help our team understand the benefits of replacing traditional grading with a standards-based report card.

Your Turn

How would you create a purpose statement, using the Case in Point or your own example?

Guiding question—

Problem framed—

Purpose statement—

Inquiry Question

Now we move on to the second part of the process, which is to develop the inquiry question. Inquiry questions are those questions that inspire us to think deeply. Inquiry questions

- ☐ should focus on an area the whole team finds interesting,

- ☐ can be answered using research,

- ☐ should not be questions the team already knows the answer to,

- ☐ will spark debate among the team,

- ☐ have one area of focus, and

- ☐ will lead the team to engage in conversations with students to understand their perspective.

Inquiry begins with a guiding question about the topic we care deeply about.

MY MODEL

Guiding question—How do we engage in more equitable grading practices?

Possible inquiry questions:

1. What do teachers believe about their own grading practices?

2. What information do teachers need to better understand standards-based grading?

3. What resources would we need to help teachers replace their traditional grading practices with standards-based grading practices?

Your Turn

How would you create inquiry questions, using the Case in Point or your own example?

Guiding question—

Possible inquiry questions:

1.

2.

3.

Theory of Action

The last step is defining your theory of action. A theory of action helps us understand how our beliefs will lead to actions that will help achieve that theory. We do this work through understanding our beliefs. One thing to keep in mind is that we need to check our beliefs. Le Fevre et al. (2019) suggest that we must "be willing to question own and others' beliefs and behavior and challenge the status quo" (p. 9). While engaging in a theory of action, we must be able to check those beliefs and assumptions.

There are many different types of theories of action, but the one I use consistently is "if . . . then" statements. The purpose here, especially when it comes to de-implementation, is to understand if our actions will lead to desired outcomes.

At the beginning of this book, I asked you to write three beliefs that you would defend when it comes to education, student learning, and school. Now I want your team to take that level of thinking and bring it to your theory of action. What strong beliefs would you defend when it comes to your area of focus?

THE RESEARCH	Killion (2003) writes, "An explicit theory of change is a roadmap for program designers, managers, participants, stakeholders, and evaluators showing how the program will work" (p. 17).

Donohoo (2013, p. 30) suggests that theories of action must fit the following criteria:

- Be committed to in writing.
- Contain causal statements that can be disproved. In a private communication (January 16, 2022) Donohoo explained, "No theory should be written in stone (or even laminated)—because we learn more as we test our theory in action, and we revise our thinking (or theories) as a result."
- Adhere to the conditions under which continuous improvement will happen.
- Include new capacities that must be developed to ensure success.

Robinson (2018) suggests,

Theories of actions have three components: the actions (behaviors), the beliefs and values that give rise to those actions, and the intended or unintended consequences of those beliefs and actions. (p. 14)

MY MODEL

Theory of Action

> **Key Beliefs**
> 1. Our traditional grading is not uniform and equitable.
> 2. Our job as educators is to make sure all students are receiving equitable grading on what they learn.
> 3. The content that teachers grade upon in the same subjects in the same grade level is vastly different.

> **Theory of Action**
> If we de-implement traditional grading and replace it with standards-based grading, then our students will have more equitable opportunities for learning.

> **Consequences**
> 1. There will be uniformity in grading.
> 2. There will be uniformity in content being covered in class.

As you can see from my example, I added three beliefs about traditional grading within the school and tied those beliefs to the "if . . . then" theory of action. Last, I defined some consequences of those actions, because there are always consequences for our actions—negative or positive. In this case we are focusing on positive consequences.

Your Turn

How would you create a theory of action, using the Case in Point or your own example?

Theory of Action

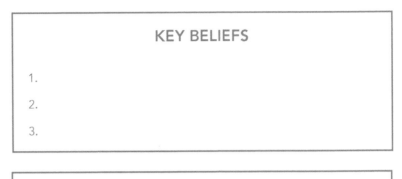

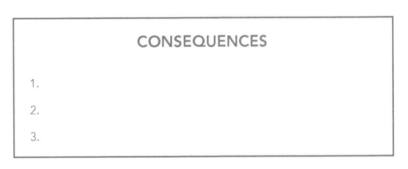

Before you can move forward as a team, it is helpful to examine whether you are making any assumptions within your theory of action. Please take a moment to review the assumptions list in Chapter 2. Do you see any such assumptions in what your team has written? If so, ask yourself what you might do to minimize those assumptions.

Evidence Collection

Part of this questioning section is to collect the evidence to understand whether the team is on the right track. This is a two-part process, and only one part will be time-consuming. Let's begin with the one that should not take long for the team, and that is deciding whether this will be a partial reduction or replacement activity. (See Figure 4.3.)

The second activity will take more time because it requires the team to collect evidence around its de-implementation focus. My example (Figure 4.4) continues to focus on grading.

Figure 4.3

	FOCUS FOR DE-IMPLEMENTATION					
CRITERIA	DE-IMPLEMENTATION EXAMPLE	PARTIAL REDUCTION	REPLACEMENT ACTION	EVIDENCE	NOTES	
The program being de-implemented has not been shown to be effective and impactful.						
The program being de-implemented is less effective or impactful than another available.	Traditional grading practices		We think we will replace traditional grading with standards-based grading.	We are reviewing research by Guskey. We have also completed empathy interviews with students and with parents.	We understand that this process could take a year. The good news is that because our team is focusing on this issue, we are already making some positive changes to our traditional grading practices that will help us transition to standards-based grading.	
The program being de-implemented causes harm.						

MY MODEL

Figure 4.4		
DE-IMPLEMENTATION FOCUS	EVIDENCE COLLECTED BY TEAM	EVIDENCE TO BE COLLECTED FROM COMMUNITY
Traditional grading versus standards-based grading	• We compared grading practices across the same content areas. • We engaged in two different book studies on standards-based grading. • Department chairs attended several professional learning opportunities focused on standards-based grading.	• Student surveys, student family surveys, and teacher surveys collected. • We engaged in several community forums/town halls with families, both in person and virtually.

Your Turn

What type of de-implementation is needed, and what evidence needs to be collected? You can use the scenario from the Case in Point or your own example. (See Figures 4.5 and 4.6 to complete your turn.)

Figure 4.5

		FOCUS FOR DE-IMPLEMENTATION			
CRITERIA	DE-IMPLEMENTATION EXAMPLE	PARTIAL REDUCTION	REPLACEMENT ACTION	EVIDENCE	NOTES
The program being de-implemented has not been shown to be effective and impactful.					
The program being de-implemented is less effective or impactful than another available.					
The program being de-implemented causes harm.					

Figure 4.6

DE-IMPLEMENTATION FOCUS	EVIDENCE COLLECTED BY TEAM	EVIDENCE TO BE COLLECTED FROM COMMUNITY

Step 2: Plan

Now that you have done your initial investigations and strategically thought through your *why* and *how*, it is time to pull it all together into one plan for the de-implementation process. This is the place for you to frame the work for all the key stakeholders in the school community to help them fully understand and engage in the process.

In this stage of the cycle of de-implementation, we plan out the most important aspects of the de-implementation process. The interesting aspect to calling them stages is that it can feel like each is an isolated activity, but the reality is that one stage flows into the next. Just like in the Tour de France, one stage sets you up nicely to do the work in the next stage. The planning tool for this is a program logic model.

The program logic model I created for my instructional leadership work, and still use to this day, is broken down into five areas:

Theory of action—What is our focus for de-implementation?

Resources—What resources do we need to be successful? This section includes the collection of evidence. Killion (2003)

THE RESEARCH

Chen et al. (1999) write, "The logic model is used to provide explanation, justifications for selecting various programmatic components and evaluation measures" (p. 449). The researchers go on to suggest that a logic model "emphasizes the importance of organizing short- and long-term goals, as well as the underlying assumptions of intervention activities as a hierarchy of objectives" (p. 450).

writes, "Data collection requires a systematic and thoughtful process to ensure that data collected are accurate and have been collected as planned" (p. 20).

Activities—What are the activities that we need to engage in for the de-implementation process? I like to keep these activities to three because any more than that may be overwhelming for the team.

Timetable—When will we begin doing the work?

Impact—What is the positive impact we want to have on students?

In Figure 4.7, I provide an example of the program logic model.

MY MODEL

As you can see from my example, I began with the theory of action and then made a list of resources that would be necessary for the process. That is followed by activities necessary to engage in de-implementation, as well as a timetable. The program logic model ends with impact, because we always want to be clear on our impact while doing this work.

Your Turn

Now it's your turn to fill in the blanks when it comes to your own program logic model (see Figure 4.8). Take your example theory of action and create your program logic model and action plan. Again, feel free to use the Case in Point or your own example.

Figure 4.7

De-implementation Program Logic Model

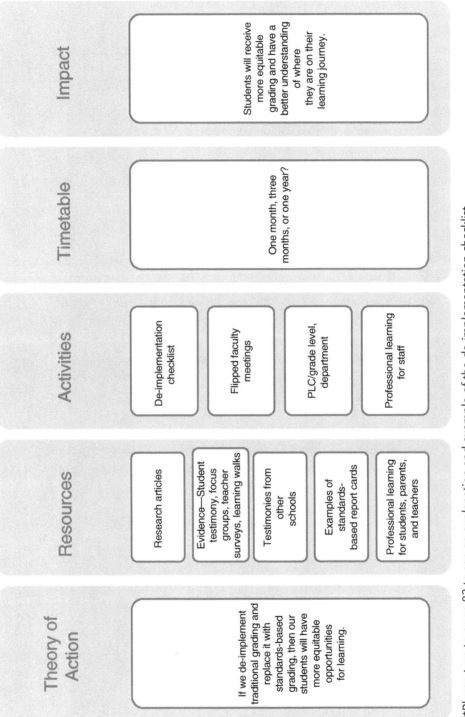

Theory of Action	Resources	Activities	Timetable	Impact
If we de-implement traditional grading and replace it with standards-based grading, then our students will have more equitable opportunities for learning.	Research articles Evidence—Student testimony, focus groups, teacher surveys, learning walks Testimonies from other schools Examples of standards-based report cards Professional learning for students, parents, and teachers	De-implementation checklist Flipped faculty meetings PLC/grade level, department Professional learning for staff	One month, three months, or one year?	Students will receive more equitable grading and have a better understanding of where they are on their learning journey.

**Please turn to page 83 to see an explanation and example of the de-implementation checklist.

Figure 4.8

De-implementation Program Logic Model

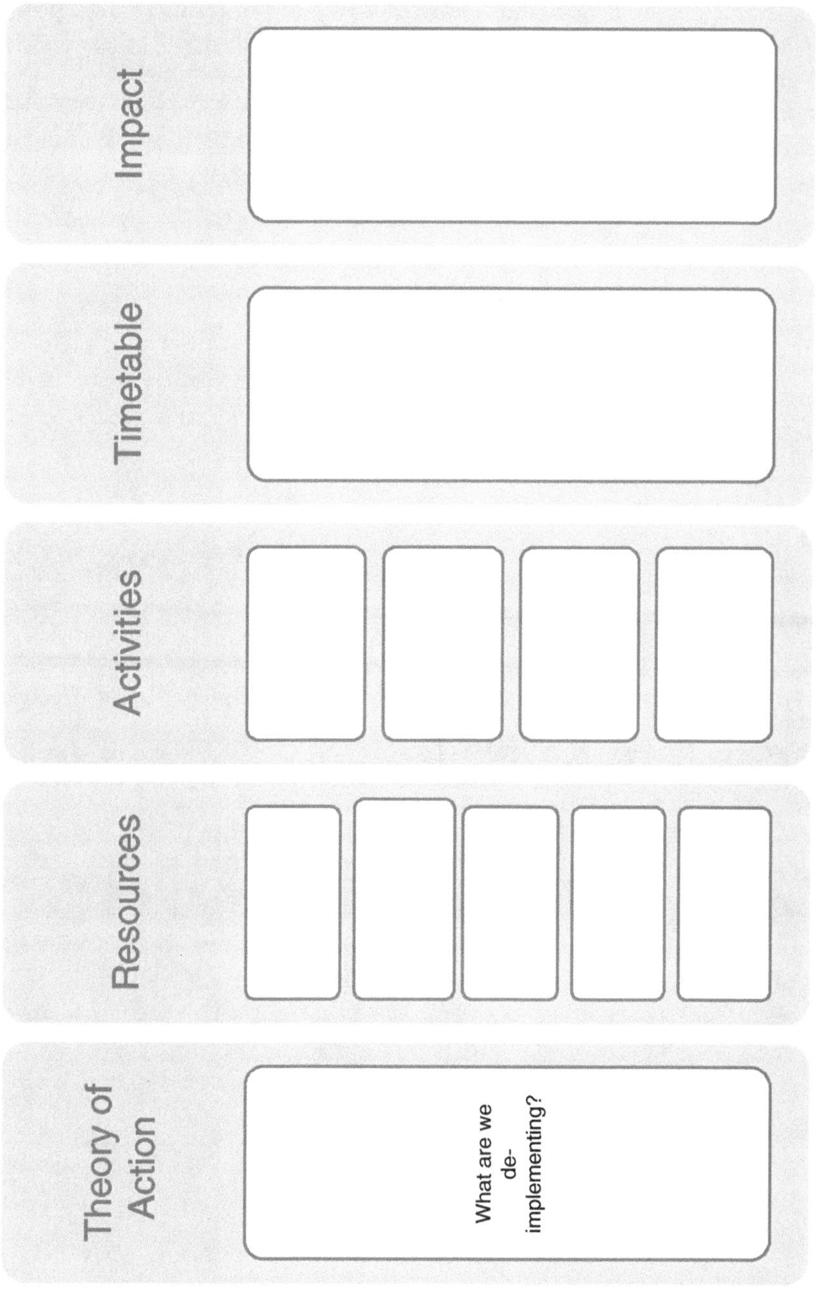

Theory of Action	Resources	Activities	Timetable	Impact
What are we de-implementing?				

Step 3: De-implement

This is the part of the process where you begin de-implementation. In Step 1, for the question section, your team collected evidence such as surveys and research. In Step 2 your team began to plan the de-implementation process, where you brainstormed ideas that would best help.

This step is about implementing the required professional learning that will help staff de-implement. That professional learning may take place during faculty meetings, after school, and in professional learning community (PLC) or department meetings.

Actions Plan

In Figure 4.9, I model what this process will look like. As you can see, I made a list of five actionable steps when engaging in the replacement action of changing grading practices. This process needs to be completed for formal partial reductions as well.

Figure 4.9

First Steps in the De-implementation Process

1. A team of teachers from across different content areas is piloting a new standards-based report card.
2. Pilot teachers will report out their progress/findings at faculty meetings. This will involve explaining how their assessments transfer to the new report card.
3. During faculty meetings, staff will further discuss grading practices by engaging in discussions around research-based articles. We know that not all staff are on board with a new report card process, and this will help flesh those issues out.
4. During mid-term and at the end of term, we will interview parents and students in pilot group and get their feedback on new report card.
5. Leaders, "teachers", and staff are engaged in site-based professional learning opportunities as well as virtual options, and being sent to regional professional learning sessions as well.

Now it's time for your team to do the same. I gave you one possibility by adding the de-implementation checklist. Please take some time to sketch out what this part of the process could look like for your team.

The De-implementation Checklist

You may have noticed in my program logic model an activity called a de-implementation checklist. The de-implementation checklist is important for many reasons, two of which are that it will help your team bring clarity to their thinking and help the team understand whether they have thought of all the necessary components to the formal de-implementation process. Before sharing your de-implementation plan with the school, it is best to complete this checklist.

When This Checklist Is Needed

Certain programs and initiatives need a team approach when it comes to de-implementation. For example, if schools are truly going to look at equitable grading practices, then there needs to be engagement among teachers and staff so they understand why this is the work for the school team. However, if a PLC is looking to de-implement a practice within a classroom, such as teacher talk versus student talk, then some of these questions on the checklist may not be applicable. In the following box, review the research behind this checklist. I have replaced the word *efficacious* with the word *impactful*. In my work, I like to use *efficacy* to focus on how a team functions.

THE RESEARCH

In the research behind de-implementation, please remember that van Bodegom-Vos et al. (2017) say de-implementation is the process of "abandoning existing low-value practices." According to Wang et al. (2018), de-implementation comes down to four areas: partial reduction, complete reversal, substitution with related replacement, and substitution with unrelated replacement of existing practice.

These have been consolidated into two areas:

- Partial reduction
- Replacement action

Farmer et al. (2021) say low-value practices are those that

- have not been shown to be effective and efficacious,
- are less effective or efficacious than another available practice,
- cause harm, or
- are no longer necessary.

De-implementation Checklist

Directions

In the de-implementation checklist, your instructional leadership team is responsible for filling out specific sections to best help you understand your next steps in the de-implementation process. Please remember, there is a difference between a formal de-implementation and an informal de-implementation (see Chapter 2). Your team will not need to complete this checklist for an informal de-implementation.

Section 1	Everyone needs to complete this section.
Section 2	Everyone needs to complete this section.
Section 3	Fill this out only if program has been shown not to be effective or impactful.
Section 4	Fill this out only if program has been shown to be less effective or impactful than another program.
Section 5	Fill this out only if program has been shown to cause harm.
Section 6	Fill this out only if program has been shown to no longer be needed.
Section 7	Fill this out only if you are a school leader.
Section 8	Fill this out only if you are part of a school team (i.e., instructional leadership team, PLC, department, etc.).
Section 9	Fill this out only if you are a teacher or staff member.
Section 10	Everyone needs to complete this section.
Section 11	Everyone needs to complete this section.

Process: As a school-based team, PLC, or department, go through each item and mark true, false, or N/A. Each set of questions is categorized for each stakeholder group within a school.

Name and brief description of practice to be de-implemented: _____

_____

_____

Section 1:

De-implementation Checklist:

In the next two statements, please choose one.

☐ This de-implementation is a partial reduction.

☐ This de-implementation is a replacement action.

Section 2:

In the next four statements, please choose one. After doing so, go to the corresponding section to complete deeper questions on the topic.

☐ The program being de-implemented has not been shown to be effective and impactful. (Go to Section 3 to continue the checklist.)

☐ The program being de-implemented is less effective or impactful than another available practice. (Go to Section 4 to continue the checklist.)

☐ The program being de-implemented causes harm. (Go to Section 5 to continue the checklist.)

☐ The program being de-implemented is no longer necessary. (Go to Section 6 to complete the checklist.)

Section 3:

The program being de-implemented has not been shown to be effective and impactful. Please answer both questions in this section and then move on to the section that corresponds with your position or context. For example, if you are a school leader, go to Section 7.

• We have collected evidence to understand that the program or initiative is not effective or impactful.

• An example of that evidence is _____

_____

Section 4:

The program being de-implemented is less effective or impactful than another available practice. Please answer both questions in this section and then move on to the section that corresponds with your context or position. For example, if you are part of an instructional leadership team, go to Section 8.

• We have collected evidence to understand that the program or initiative is less effective or impactful than another available program.

• We are confident the other program will be more effective because _____

_____

Section 5 :

The program being de-implemented causes harm. Please answer both questions in this section and then move on to the section that corresponds with your context or position.

For example, if you are a teacher or staff member and part of a PLC or department, go to Section 9.

- We have collected evidence to understand that the program or initiative causes harm.

- We understand the program causes harm because _____

_____

Section 6:

The program being de-implemented is no longer necessary. Please answer both questions in this section and then move on to the section that corresponds with your context or position. For example, if you are a teacher or staff member and part of a PLC or department, go to Section 9.

- We have collected sufficient evidence to understand that the program or initiative is no longer necessary.

- We are confident the program is no longer necessary because _____

_____

Section 7:

School Leader:

- We have collected evidence to understand whether the program or initiative was impactful, causes harm, or is no longer necessary.

- Our teachers/staff understand the definition of de-implementation when it comes to this program or initiative.

- I have done a sufficient job focusing on de-implementation in staff/faculty meetings when it comes to this program or initiative.

- I understand the resources, or I am fully supportive of providing the resources my teachers/staff need for this de-implementation process to be successful.

- I understand that we need to evaluate how successful this de-implementation process has been.

Section 8:

Team:

This section can be viewed as a school-based team, PLC, or department.

- As a team we have considered why de-implementation is the action we are taking.

- We have considered specific goals when it comes to de-implementation.

- Those goals are:
  - ○ We have exhausted all possibilities of implementing this program in the first place.
  - ○ We will engage in a cycle of de-implementation.
  - ○ We have considered the evidence we can collect to understand how de-implementation is progressing.

Section 9:

Teachers/Staff:

- Teachers/staff understand that we are de-implementing the program or initiative.
- Teachers/staff have been involved through stakeholder engagement when it comes to how this de-implementation will look.

Section 10:

Students:

- Students have a voice in the de-implementation process.
- Students understand why we have chosen to de-implement this program or initiative.

Section 11:

Community:

When it comes to the community, we can look at this as our board of education: families of students within our individual classrooms or grade levels. For example, if schools are changing their grading practices from traditional to standards-based report cards, the community understands why this is necessary. If teachers are incorporating collaboration into their classrooms to promote student voice, families within the classroom understand why this is happening. Schools looking to build communication understand the importance of these next statements.

- The community understands the concept of de-implementation.
- The community fully supports the de-implementation of this program or initiative.
- We have taken time to understand the opinions of the community when de-implementing this program or initiative.

Step 4: Evaluate

The last step in this process is to evaluate if the de-implementation is working. Hattie (2012) writes, "So often the evaluation is in terms such as 'It worked for me', 'The students seem to enjoy it', 'The students appeared engaged', or 'It allowed me to get through the curriculum'" (p. 84). Hattie goes on to say, "School leaders and systems must take the lead in this evaluation process, and create a safe and rewarding environment in which the evaluation process can occur" (p. 167).

Evaluating impact using evidence is part of the process. In Figure 4.12, you will see an evidence-gathering tool I created. It's meant to be a simple template to help us understand how effective the partial reduction or replacement action has been when it comes to student learning. I created this one around the standards-based grading theory of action.

Figure 4.10 provides examples of possible evidence that the instructional leadership team could collect. Remember that there is a balance

Figure 4.10

THEORY OF ACTION EVIDENCE		
IF WE DE-IMPLEMENT TRADITIONAL GRADING AND REPLACE IT WITH STANDARDS-BASED GRADING, THEN OUR STUDENTS WILL HAVE MORE EQUITABLE OPPORTUNITIES FOR LEARNING.	DIRECT EVIDENCE	INDIRECT EVIDENCE
Leadership Action—Examples: focus groups, surveys, examples of standards-based report cards from across the school		
Teacher Action—examples of their standards-based report cards, student portfolios tied to standards		
Student Action—Examples: student-led conference, artifact chosen by student		

between uniformity and creativity. What I mean is that not everything the teachers provide as evidence must look the same. There is space for creativity. We often hear the loose–tight analogy, which means that we must be tight with our focus but can be loose with how we encourage people to get there.

For example, standards-based grading must be tight to provide less room for error and more of an opportunity for students to receive equitable grading. How teachers engage in teaching the standards can be the loose part because it may include anything from direct instruction to project-based learning. However, don't ask for so much evidence that it becomes a huge burden on teachers and students.

Your Turn

What evidence could you collect for the Case in Point or your own example? (See Figure 4.11.)

Sometimes Slow Is Fast

I understand this can be a challenging process when going through it for the first time, but there is a cost when we hurry and jump into

Figure 4.11

THEORY OF ACTION EVIDENCE		
WHAT IS YOUR THEORY OF ACTION?	DIRECT EVIDENCE	INDIRECT EVIDENCE
Leadership Action—		
Teacher Action—		
Student Action—		

initiatives. I am asking you to slow down because we know that slowing down helps us think more clearly. If you are looking for perfection in this process, you will not find it. It's important not to get caught up in the exact language. It's more important to get caught up in making sure the practices we have in place are effective and efficient.

Anticipating Roadblocks

People struggle with focusing on one area of concern. There are so many distractions that come to us as educators. Over the years I have been practicing meditation, I have come to realize how active our minds are, and how much distraction gets in the way of our progress.

To do the work that de-implementation requires of us, it's important for your team to have a conversation about overconsumption and the need for focus. We are constantly being bombarded with ideas that are marketing themselves to us as the next best thing, and sometimes we do not even understand how much it happens. We should work as a team to tune out that noise and focus on one area to formally de-implement.

TIPS TO CONSIDER

- Make sure that everyone on the team has a voice in choosing the area to de-implement.

- Discuss the role of overconsumption in our lives and how that intersects with the choices we make in our classrooms and schools, as well as the actions we take. This has everything to do with the initiative fatigue we feel in school.

- Make sure that there are at least two people designated to keep the team focused. It does not have to be the school leader, but there should be two people so no one person feels as though they are the wet blanket on the team.

Monitoring Our Minds: Filling the Void

Too often, we try to fill a void in our lives by going out and buying something new, and then we find that the new thing we bought filled the void only for a few fleeting moments. What we should do is look within to find what we already have and see how that can satisfy those moments of need.

For example, when I was eleven years old, my dad passed away after a three-year battle with cancer. A couple of years later, all my four older siblings had moved out of the house to begin their lives as adults. What that meant was that my mom and I had to figure out how to live in a house of two as opposed to a house of seven. To deal with the loss, my mother and I spent lots of time at the mall, where she bought countless gifts—even though we were on a limited income. As an adult, when I was bored or feeling low, I found myself buying new clothes or devices I did not need but desperately wanted at the time. Then one day it dawned on me that I never seemed to be satisfied.

For me, monitoring my mind means looking within to see what I have that is already useful. I think school teams need to do the same work. What I want for your team to understand is that you may not need all the stuff around you as much as you need each other to focus on areas of impact and to use the process laid out in this chapter to help strengthen those areas of impact.

The hope is that this process of de-implementation will help you find clarity in your work, that you will spend less time worrying about work because your actions are impactful and bring confidence. Less time worrying means more time being present in our personal lives. De-implementation is that important.

In the End

The cycle of de-implementation is a necessary component of the de-implementation process. I know what many of you are thinking: My example of standards-based grading seems like more of an implementation than a de-implementation, but I wanted to model an example that might require the most work. Undoing one activity and replacing it with a new activity will almost always come with the most challenges. All other types of de-implementation action will take less time.

The cycle of de-implementation, program logic model, and de-implementation checklist are meant to help your teachers, staff, and leaders be more intentional about what they do in your school, even if that means they do less of whatever that is to create a space to really practice well-being and stress reduction.

In the next chapter, I will provide some more food for thought around teams and pacing. This is also where your instructional leadership team can fully engage in the formal de-implementation process using all the templates I introduced in this chapter. There are also blank templates in the back of the book that you can print repeatedly.

DISCUSSION QUESTIONS

1. What is beneficial about the cycle of de-implementation process?

2. What is challenging about the cycle of de-implementation process?

3. Is there any part of it you would not use again?

4. What are your thoughts on it being called de-implementation, even though one of the aspects is to engage in a replacement action?

What is resonating with you right now?

Your Team's De-implementation Process

(considering who you need and how fast to go)

5

Replace district-driven PD with staff-driven professional development. My staff are professionals, and they need to be treated this way; we need to allow them to determine what they need and collectively allow them to grow their own professional development.

—Anonymous

SUCCESS CRITERIA

By the end of this chapter, you will be able to do the following:

- Engage in your own de-implementation process

- Hopefully find a better work/life balance

Write two of your own success criteria:

-

-

In the Survey Monkey I created to get feedback from educators when it comes to de-implementation, one of the questions I asked was, "What is your interest in de-implementation?"

The top two answers (from a list of stock answers) were "Looking for a deeper impact on student learning" and "I don't think everything I do is effective, and I'd like to solely focus on effective practices." I also included a space for them to add their own ideas, but no one did. What that means for me here, with this small sample of data, is that despite challenges and stress, most educators who take time to fill out surveys are more concerned about impact than anything else. This is the good news for a team about to engage in de-implementation.

This Chapter

The first half of this chapter will focus on your team and their strengths, agendas, and pacing for de-implementing initiatives. The second half will provide a space for you to plan once your team officially decides which big initiative they will tackle first. Remember, for smaller roll-backs the formal cycle is not needed. Here are some indicators that you and your team will need the formal cycle:

- This change requires a team.
- This change impacts most of the school.
- This change requires data collection from a variety of sources.
- It could take many months to see a result.

Part I: Your Team

"You need to have a cohesive team who can engage with one another, even if that means challenging one another's thinking."

To do this work of de-implementation, you must be a part of a team where you have a role and a voice. You need to have a cohesive team who can engage with one another, even if that means challenging one another's thinking. Remember that when we started the inquiry process, a key ingredient was developing an inquiry question that might spark debate. The work is too important for passivity. Additionally, your team will no doubt engage in a discussion about the culture of the school, because the improvements you are considering making are ones that have been embedded in the culture for a long time.

I have used grading as one of my primary examples throughout the book, and grading is one of the topics that has deep cultural implications. According to Fullan (2007), school culture can be defined as the guiding beliefs and values that are clear in how the school operates. Whether you are leading a school in Australia or the United Kingdom, where you are part of a system of schools rather than a school system, or leading in a greater school system like in the United States or Canada, if there is a lack of shared beliefs around the improvement your team is making, this work of de-implementation may take longer than in communities where the culture has a shared set of beliefs.

At the beginning of each chapter, I provided you with a Case in Point from my own experiences as a teacher, leadership coach, and facilitator of workshops. Now it's your turn. How would you describe your team's relationship?

CASE IN POINT

Your Team's Dynamics

_____

_____

_____

_____

_____

_____

_____

_____

_____

_____

_____

_____

_____

_____

CLUTTER CHECK

I want you to declutter and remember those teams that were most impactful. Think of a team you enjoyed being a part of and you felt had great synergy. Consider the following questions:

- What made the team so impactful?

- What roles did each person have on the team?

- What challenges did you face, and how did you overcome them?

- What improvements did you take on when it came to student learning?

- How did you stay focused on one area and not get sidetracked by other shiny new toys?

The Mindset of Each Member

Your team must have the necessary mindset to move forward. There are a few essential elements to maintaining that mindset. In an *Education Week* article, Hill (2021) writes that individuals on the team need these ingredients:

- *Will—literally whether teachers decide to embrace new practices or materials or to shelve them*

- *Skill—whether teachers have the knowledge and expertise to implement a given program*

- *Organizational capacity—whether an organization has in place tools, routines, and relationships that enable implementation*

- *Contexts and coherence—whether the program will work given its particulars and the local setting's needs, strengths, and weaknesses*

> "De-implementation is about taking our control back in an effort to provide a deeper learning experience for students, and that requires the input of each member of the instructional leadership team."

What is important about this process, and perhaps at the heart of it, is again to provide staff with a voice. Just as described in the opening quotation for this chapter, leaders and staff often feel that things are done to them and not with them. If that person felt their teachers had a voice in the district-driven professional learning conversation, they would probably feel less resistant to it. De-implementation is about taking our control back in an effort to provide a deeper learning experience for students, and that requires the input of each member of the instructional leadership team.

MORE ON PRODUCTIVE TEAMS . . .

In my collective leader efficacy work (DeWitt, 2021), I defined eight drivers necessary to do this work:

Mindset—Do members of the team have a deficit mindset or a growth mindset?

Well-being—What practices can the team engage in to help them do their work more effectively? This involves looking at how team members talk with one another during the process and setting up work/life boundaries.

Professional learning and development—How does the team learn together?

Working conditions—Areas such as workload and school climate are included here. It's where I began talking about de-implementation.

Organizational commitment—How are members of the organization committed to student learning?

Context beliefs—Do the members of the team believe that their organization will support them when they try to be innovative (Leithwood & Janzti, 2008)? Many members of a team often feel that they cannot voice their true opinions. This needs to be corrected for de-implementation to really work.

Skills to work in collectives—Slavin (2010) writes, "For achievement outcomes, positive results depend on two key factors. One is the presence of group goals, the other is individual accountability" (p. 161). For de-implementation to work, the group needs a common goal, but members of the team need to take accountability for pursuing that goal.

Confidence to work in collectives—Bandura (1997) found that there are four experiences that help develop our confidence: (1) mastery experiences, (2) vicarious experiences, (3) verbal persuasion, and (4) affective states. Through these experiences we develop the confidence to ensure that we contribute to the group during the de-implementation process.

Flexible Methods

When engaging in this work as a team, use a hybrid approach so your team can do their best thinking. Use Google Docs and Mentimeter to engage with one another. I can imagine that you have some meetings in a remote setting. Perhaps you use an anonymous online engagement tool like Mentimeter, where you take Guskey's questions and break them down one by one so people can record their responses anonymously. Have fun with the work, because your meetings around it may be one of the few times you get to talk about teaching and learning.

Pacing and Agendas

The following sample agenda (Figure 5.2) and pacing guides are based on an instructional leadership team that meets for ninety minutes two times a month. Additionally, you will notice on the agenda that I have included a place to assign roles such as those suggested below in Figure 5.1. When developing collective leader efficacy among a school leadership team, which is a shared conviction that they will work together and have a positive impact on student learning, I ask teams to develop roles for each member. Those roles, except for that of co-chair, can change from meeting to meeting depending on the topic and fluidity of the team. Co-chairs are often the same two teachers for the whole year, and the school building leader is a member of the team who can take on a role like researcher or facilitator of learning.

Figure 5.1

SUGGESTIONS FOR TEAM ROLES	
Co-chairs	Two people are in charge of leading the management side of the instructional leadership meeting.
Facilitator of learning	This person, who does not need to be the same person at each session, facilitates the learning for a specific session.
Sketchnoting	Visuals are an impactful method of capturing the thoughts and actions of the instructional leadership team.
Researcher	One or more people can take on the role of researching student engagement, instructional strategies, or some other aspect of the instructional core goal the group is taking on.
Notetaker	This is an old-school job, but it is an important one.
Critical friend	These members of the team can provide important understanding of why some in the school may not want to focus on particular goals.
Innovator	This person doesn't see just what is; they see all the possibilities of what could be.

Sample Agenda

Figure 5.2

ILT Meeting

Date:

Establish roles for this meeting

01   **Roles**
_____

Co-chairs–

Facilitator of Learning–

Sketchnoting–

Researcher–

Notetaker–

Critical friend–

Innovator–

02   **Develop Success Criteria for the meeting**

- How will we know we are successful at the end of today's meeting?

03   **Management Issues**

- 20 minutes to discuss management issues

04

- Continue de-implementation process

Pacing

Pacing is important for the de-implementation process. In the figures below, I have provided possible pacing for de-implementing a couple of practices. However, I want to be cautious as I offer this pacing guide because in my experience as a coach working with leaders, and as a school building leader myself, what might work for one team may not work for another. Additionally, COVID taught us all about how new challenges can come any day, so this pacing guide is offered up as a reference but not a hard-and-fast rule. For instance, many times classroom pacing guides take teachers from the beginning of the unit to the end, but when we are focusing on de-implementation, it's important to be flexible as we go through the year.

For example, in the state work I do with the Washington Association of School Administrators (WASA), Mike Nelson, Chris Beals, Jenni Donohoo, and I make sure we have the success criteria for our two-year journey, and we set up learning opportunities for a few months in advance. But we also make sure we ask for feedback from the more than 180 directors of teaching and learning across the state, to make sure our learning opportunities are connected to their individual and team theories of action.

Broad Timelines

As a rule of thumb, de-implementing a practice without adopting a new one will take less time than adopting a replacement practice, such as the grading example in Chapter 4. Furthermore, partially reducing a practice will take less time than most replacement actions. Additionally, when a school engages in a replacement action, that decision does not happen overnight. Most times a replacement action comes from a conversation the school community has been involved in for years but has not acted on yet.

Given those two ideas, pacing for a partial reduction is most likely going to be different from pacing for a replacement action. I have provided two figures below: One focuses on a partial reduction when it comes to teacher talk versus student talk. You may remember that was one of my examples in the partial reduction section in a previous chapter. The other focuses on a replacement action, which is standards-based grading, also used as an example throughout the book.

First let's begin with the partial reduction. In Figure 5.3, you will notice that the process begins in September, which is the first or second month

Figure 5.3

PACING GUIDE FOR TEACHER TALK

	INITIAL BRAINSTORMING	DE-IMPLEMENTATION FOCUS	INQUIRING	PLANNING	DE-IMPLEMENTING	EVALUATING	MAINTAINING
September	School leadership team develops a common understanding of what de-implementation means. Team creates a top ten list of areas to de-implement and narrows list down to seven.						
October	Team gets feedback from staff/teachers on top seven.	Team chooses to focus on teacher talk versus student talk to increase student engagement.					

(Continued)

Figure 5.3   (Continued)

| | PACING GUIDE FOR TEACHER TALK | | | | | |
	INITIAL BRAINSTORMING	DE-IMPLEMENTATION FOCUS	INQUIRING	PLANNING	DE-IMPLEMENTING	EVALUATING	MAINTAINING
November			School leadership teams develop a theory of action, which is shared with teachers across the school in PLCs.	At faculty meeting, teachers and leaders develop a plan to partially reduce teacher talk.			
December				At faculty and PLC meetings, teachers develop an understanding of engaging in collaborative learning models that impact student learning.	Faculty focus on two different collaborative student models and begin partially reducing talk within the classroom.	Teachers evaluate impact of action through student exit surveys.	
January						Teachers bring evidence to January faculty meeting.	Teachers continue to use two or three collaborative models. Collect evidence to understand impact.
February							Teachers share evidence at February faculty meeting.

for most schools in North America. Inquiring, planning, de-implementing, and evaluating are part of our cycle of inquiry. Additionally, I mention evidence collection. I am a proponent of flipped faculty meetings, where staff must engage in some prep work prior to the meeting and then engage in active learning around evidence during their faculty meeting.

In Figure 5.4 (pages 104–105), we must engage in a pacing chart that is a bit longer because we are focusing on a replacement action. That replacement action is moving from traditional grading to standards-based grading. Standards-based grading is one of those topics we know schools engage in for a long time before they begin the process. You will note in Figure 5.4 that year one is all about initially brainstorming what it will look like and creating a pilot group to find the best standards-based report card.

In Figure 5.5 (pages 106–107), you will notice that year two is when the staff begin using standards-based report cards. Included in this pacing guide is the de-implementation process, evaluation, and maintenance, which we learned about from PRISM in Chapter 1, which focused on implementation.

How do you prefer to create a pacing schedule for your initiatives? As a principal, I always felt compelled to plan out the whole year to show that I thought deeply about every part of it. However, my mindset has changed there, because now I prefer to plan out the first few months and then reflect and process how it is all going before taking next steps.

What is your process? Do you plan out the year? Or do you plan for half the year and leave it open to evolve into something you haven't planned?

CLUTTER CHECK

Part II: Your Official Cycle of De-implementation

In this part, there will be little narrative from me as you go through the process. The chapters leading up to this one are where I offered most of my guidance. Return to the first activity in the book, where you wrote down three beliefs. Remember as we went through the

Figure 5.4

PACING GUIDE FOR GRADING (YEAR ONE)			
	INITIAL BRAINSTORMING	TEACHER AND STAFF INPUT	PILOT GROUP PLANNING
Summer	School leadership team solely focus on grading. No need for a top ten list.		
September		School leadership team share their focus with staff and ask for a group of teachers across content area to pilot de-implementation.	
October			Pilot group meets with school leadership team to discuss options for standards-based grading.
November			Pilot group engages in professional learning (i.e., site-based, virtual, in-person conferences) that focus on standards-based grading.
December			Pilot group meets with neighboring schools that use standards-based grading.
January			Pilot group narrows down to two different report cards.

PACING GUIDE FOR GRADING (YEAR ONE)

	INITIAL BRAINSTORMING	TEACHER AND STAFF INPUT	PILOT GROUP PLANNING
February			Parents/students in pilot group receive professional learning.
March			Pilot teachers begin using standards-based reporting.
April			Pilot teachers receive professional learning on how to use standards-based reporting, using a competency-based learning approach where they bring evidence to professional learning.
May			All teachers begin engaging in professional learning focusing on standards-based reporting and report cards.
June/Summer			Pilot teachers narrow down to one standards-based report card. Begin planning for teacher professional learning for next school year.

Figure 5.5

PACING GUIDE FOR GRADING (YEAR TWO)

	DE-IMPLEMENT	EVALUATE	MAINTAIN
Summer	Teachers receive professional learning on standards-based report card. They develop their own theory of action and cycle of inquiry. Teachers are paid for summer work.		
August/September	Teachers begin using standards-based reporting. Engage in a cycle of inquiry as a department or PLC.	Teachers evaluate the impact of standards-based reporting on student learning.	Teachers receive professional learning (i.e., site-based, virtual, PLC, workshop) on standards-based reporting.
October	Teachers continue standards-based reporting. Engage in a cycle of inquiry as a department or PLC.	Teachers evaluate the impact of standards-based reporting on student learning in their PLC or department.	Teachers continue to receive professional learning (i.e., site-based, virtual, PLC, workshop) on standards-based reporting.
November	Teachers continue standards-based reporting. Engage in a cycle of inquiry as a department or PLC.	Teachers evaluate the impact of standards-based reporting on student learning in their PLC or department.	Teachers continue to receive professional learning (i.e., site-based, virtual, PLC, workshop) on standards-based reporting.
December	Teachers continue standards-based reporting. Engage in a cycle of inquiry as a department or PLC.	Teachers evaluate the impact of standards-based reporting on student learning in their PLC or department.	Teachers continue to receive professional learning (i.e., site-based, virtual, PLC, workshop) on standards-based reporting.

PACING GUIDE FOR GRADING (YEAR TWO)

	DE-IMPLEMENT	EVALUATE	MAINTAIN
January	Teachers continue standards-based reporting. Engage in a cycle of inquiry as a department or PLC.	Teachers evaluate the impact of standards-based reporting on student learning in their PLC or department.	Teachers continue to receive professional learning (i.e., site-based, virtual, PLC, workshop) on standards-based reporting.
February	Teachers continue standards-based reporting. Engage in a cycle of inquiry as a department or PLC.	Teachers evaluate the impact of standards-based reporting on student learning in their PLC or department.	Teachers continue to receive professional learning (i.e., site-based, virtual, PLC, workshop) on standards-based reporting.
March	Teachers continue standards-based reporting. Engage in a cycle of inquiry as a department or PLC.	Teachers evaluate the impact of standards-based reporting on student learning in their PLC or department.	Teachers continue to receive professional learning (i.e., site-based, virtual, PLC, workshop) on standards-based reporting.
April	Teachers continue standards-based reporting. Engage in a cycle of inquiry as a department or PLC.	Teachers evaluate the impact of standards-based reporting on student learning in their PLC or department.	Teachers continue to receive professional learning (i.e., site-based, virtual, PLC, workshop) on standards-based reporting.
May	Teachers continue standards-based reporting. Engage in a cycle of inquiry as a department or PLC.	Teachers evaluate the impact of standards-based reporting on student learning in their PLC or department.	Teachers continue to receive professional learning (i.e., site-based, virtual, PLC, workshop) on standards-based reporting.
June/Summer		Teachers, students, and families help evaluate year one of the new report card process.	

chapters, I asked you to establish a connection between those beliefs and your top ten list of what you would de-implement. We then trimmed that list to seven. Now is the time to focus on just one big area. What is it?

Our one area of focus is

_____.

Figure 5.6 once again illustrates the steps in the cycle of de-implementation.

Figure 5.6

Cycle of De-implementation

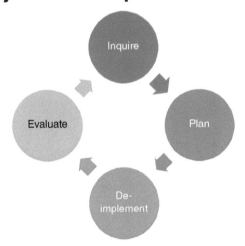

Step 1—Inquire

What area did you write above when it comes to the formal de-implementation process? As you did with the practice section in Chapter 4, please take time to develop a guiding question, frame the problem, and then develop a purpose statement. Remember that the guiding question focuses on the issue you are trying to solve.

Guiding question:

At this point, your team will take that guiding question and create a problem statement around it, using anecdotal or empirical evidence to frame it.

Problem framed:

Purpose statement:

Now we move on to the second part of the process, which is to develop the inquiry question. Take your guiding question from above and create two or three possible inquiry questions as you did in the practice section in Chapter 4.

Inquiry question:

Guiding question:

Possible inquiry questions:
-
-
-

Now that you have your inquiry questions, your team needs to define some key beliefs around this focus. In Chapter 4 I highlighted how important key beliefs are, and now it is your turn to address your team's key beliefs.

How was the conversation about key beliefs? Did you learn anything about the people around the table? What were some of the most important aspects of the conversation? Did you thank one another for being vulnerable? Has it been a safe place to do this work?

Evidence Collection

Part of this questioning section is to collect the evidence to understand whether the team is on the right track.

Theory of Action

KEY BELIEFS
1.
2.
3.

THEORY OF ACTION

CONSEQUENCES
1.
2.
3.

FOCUS FOR DE-IMPLEMENTATION

CRITERIA	DE-IMPLEMENTATION EXAMPLE	PARTIAL REDUCTION	REPLACEMENT ACTION	EVIDENCE	NOTES
The program being de-implemented has not been shown to be effective and impactful.					
The program being de-implemented is less effective or impactful than another available.					
The program being de-implemented causes harm.					

DE-IMPLEMENTATION FOCUS	EVIDENCE COLLECTED BY TEAM	EVIDENCE TO BE COLLECTED FROM COMMUNITY

Program Logic Model: De-implementation

Theory of Action	Resources	Activities	Timetable	Impact on Student/ Teachers
What are we de-implementing?				

Step 2—Plan

We now move on to planning and de-implementing the initiative. Take your theory of action from above and plug it into the program logic model template below or from the back of the book.

What are the resources necessary to do this work? What activities will your instructional leadership team engage in for this de-implementation? What is your timetable? Depending on the focus for your de-implementation, this could last one month, three months, or a whole year.

Last, what impact will this de-implementation have on students and teachers in the school community?

Step 3—De-implement

This brings us to de-implementation. Just as in Chapter 4, I began the actionable steps section for you by writing the de-implementation checklist.

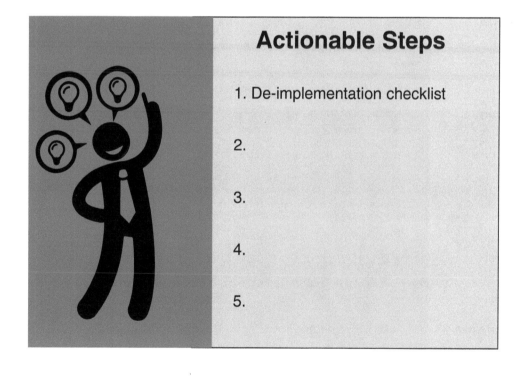

Actionable Steps

1. De-implementation checklist

2.

3.

4.

5.

De-implementation Checklist

Directions

In the de-implementation checklist, your instructional leadership team is responsible for filling out specific sections to best help you understand your next steps in the de-implementation process. Please remember, there is a difference between a formal de-implementation and an informal de-implementation. Your team will not need to complete this checklist for an informal de-implementation.

Section 1	Everyone needs to complete this section.
Section 2	Everyone needs to complete this section.
Section 3	Fill this out only if program has been shown to not be effective or impactful.
Section 4	Fill this out only if program has been shown to be less effective or impactful than another program.
Section 5	Fill this out only if program has been shown to cause harm.
Section 6	Fill this out only if program has been shown to no longer be needed.
Section 7	Fill this out only if you are a school leader.
Section 8	Fill this out only if you are part of a school team (i.e., instructional leadership team, PLC, department, etc.).
Section 9	Fill this out only if you are a teacher or staff member.
Section 10	Everyone needs to complete this section.
Section 11	Everyone needs to complete this section.

In the research behind de-implementation, please remember that van Bodegom-Vos et al. (2017) say de-implementation is the process of "abandoning existing low-value practices."

According to Wang et al. (2018), de-implementation comes down to four areas:

- Partial reduction
- Complete reversal
- Substitution with related replacement
- Substitution with unrelated replacement of existing practice

Remember that we have consolidated that important research into two areas:

- Partial reduction

- Replacement action

Farmer et al. (2021) say low-value practices are those that

- have not been shown to be effective and efficacious,

- are less effective or efficacious than another available practice,

- cause harm, or

- are no longer necessary.

Also remember that we have replaced the word *efficacious* with the word *impactful*. In my work, I like to use *efficacy* to focus on how a team functions. The checklist below considers those research-based areas of de-implementation.

Process: As a school-based team, PLC, or department, go through each item and mark true, false, or N/A. Each set of questions is categorized for each stakeholder group within a school.

Name and brief description of practice to be de-implemented: _____

_____

_____

Section 1

De-implementation Checklist:

In the next two statements, please choose one.

- This de-implementation is a partial reduction.

- This de-implementation is a replacement action.

Section 2

In the next four statements, please choose one. After doing so, go to the corresponding section to complete deeper questions on the topic.

- The program being de-implemented has not been shown to be effective and impactful. (Go to Section 3 to continue the checklist.)

- The program being de-implemented is less effective or impactful than another available practice. (Go to Section 4 to continue the checklist.)

- The program being de-implemented causes harm. (Go to Section 5 to continue the checklist.)

- The program being de-implemented is no longer necessary. (Go to Section 6 to complete the checklist.)

Section 3

The program being de-implemented has not been shown to be effective and impactful. Please answer both questions in this section and then move on to the section that corresponds with your position or context. For example, if you are a school leader, go to Section 7.

- We have collected evidence to understand that the program or initiative is not effective or impactful.

- An example of that evidence is _____

_____

Section 4

The program being de-implemented is less effective or impactful than another available practice. Please answer both questions in this section and then move on to the section that corresponds with your context or position. For example, if you are part of an instructional leadership team, go to Section 8.

- We have collected evidence to understand that the program or initiative is less effective or impactful than another available program.

- We are confident the other program will be more effective because _____

_____

Section 5

The program being de-implemented causes harm. Please answer both questions in this section and then move on to the section that corresponds with your context or position. For example, if you are a teacher or staff member and part of a PLC or department, go to Section 9.

- We have collected evidence to understand that the program or initiative causes harm.

- We understand the program causes harm because _____

_____

Section 6

The program being de-implemented is no longer necessary. Please answer both questions in this section and then move on to the section that corresponds with your context or position. For example, if you are a teacher or staff member and part of a PLC or department, go to Section 9.

- We have collected sufficient evidence to understand that the program or initiative is no longer necessary.

- We are confident the program is no longer necessary because _____

_____

Section 7

School Leader:

- We have collected evidence to understand whether the program or initiative was efficacious, causes harm, or is no longer necessary.

- Our teachers/staff understand the definition of de-implementation when it comes to this program or initiative.

- I have done a sufficient job focusing on de-implementation in staff/faculty meetings when it comes to this program or initiative.

- I understand the resources, or I am fully supportive of providing the resources my teachers/staff need for this de-implementation process to be successful.

- I understand that we need to evaluate how successful this de-implementation process has been.

Section 8

Team:

This section can be viewed as a school-based team, PLC, or department.

- As a team we have considered why de-implementation is the action we are taking.

- We have considered specific goals when it comes to de-implementation.

- Those goals are:

- We have exhausted all possibilities of implementing this program in the first place.

- We will engage in a cycle of de-implementation approach when engaging in de-implementation.

- We have considered the evidence we can collect to understand how de-implementation is progressing.

Section 9

Teachers/Staff:

- Teachers/staff understand that we are de-implementing the program or initiative.
- Teachers/staff have been involved through stakeholder engagement when it comes to how this de-implementation will look.

Section 10

Students:

- Students have a voice in the de-implementation process.
- Students understand why we have chosen to de-implement this program or initiative.

Section 11

Community:

When it comes to the community, we can look at this as our board of education: families of students within our individual classrooms or grade levels. For example, if schools are changing their grading practices from traditional to standards-based report cards, the community understands why this is necessary. If teachers are incorporating collaboration into their classroom to promote student voice, families within the classroom understand why this is happening. Schools looking to build communication understand the importance of these next statements.

- The community understands the concept of de-implementation.
- The community fully supports the de-implementation of this program or initiative.
- We have taken time to understand the opinions of the community when de-implementing this program or initiative.

Step 4—Evaluate

As a team, you need to decide what evidence you should collect to understand the impact of your de-implementation actions. In the template below or the one offered in the back of the book, write down the evidence you would like to collect. Try not to overwhelm one another with numerous pieces of evidence.

THEORY OF ACTION EVIDENCE		
WHAT IS YOUR THEORY OF ACTION?	**DIRECT EVIDENCE**	**INDIRECT EVIDENCE**
Leadership Action—		
Teacher Action—		
Student Action—		

Anticipating Roadblocks

It is important to note that teachers are being asked to engage in a cycle of inquiry within their PLCs or departments. They will be required to develop a theory of action as a team. What we know is that not all teachers will be on board with this, and there will be PLCs or departments that will struggle with the process. I wrote about those issues within my book *Collective Leader Efficacy: Strengthening Instructional Leadership Teams*. My point here is not to get you to purchase that book while you read this one; it is for you to understand that I do know this will be challenging work for your team and school community. You will be hit with other challenges along the way, which we all learned from COVID, but it's important to try to maintain focus on your one replacement action in the de-implementation process, which is what I did in this chapter when I offered the pacing guide example about standards-based report cards.

Monitoring Our Minds: Well-Being

Over the past few years there has been a lot of talk about well-being, but it's been mostly lip service. I'm sorry if that sounds somewhat harsh, but as I said at the beginning of the book, we are in a crisis in our schools here and around the world. Leaders and teachers are asked to do more with less and to give more and more of their time. You must monitor your mind and realize that if your team doesn't begin setting boundaries, this issue with workload and stress will only get worse. One of those boundaries should be to maintain a focus on one area of de-implementation. What this means is that if your focus is on a large topic like grading, then you must be okay with saying no to other large opportunities that may arise. Don't begin a focus on grading and then say yes to another large initiative like redeveloping your PLC process at the same time. Use the current PLC structure to engage in a cycle of inquiry around your replacement action.

Another note about well-being: In my examples, I had a pilot group that engaged in standards-based grading. Too often the members of those groups are spread thin and find themselves on multiple committees because they are our worker bees. Do not overwhelm them. A replacement action like grading is a challenging undertaking, so allow those people to set boundaries when it comes to the number of committees they sit on.

There is a saying that made the rounds on social media: "If givers don't set boundaries, the takers around them never will." It's time to set boundaries, but additionally, it's time to change the mindset that doing more is better, because impact doesn't happen from doing more. Impact happens only when your team engages in the right work, stays focused on that work, and de-implements practices that take them away from doing that work.

In the End

One of the biggest challenges to all this work is that people don't know where to start. I recommend beginning with partial reductions where the results can be seen in a relatively short amount of time. A quick win could help fuel the fire of trimming away any activities that do not align with your goals. Then take the time to focus your attentions on larger efforts that require a formal cycle of de-implementation. The bigger the change is, the more you will need the cycle to make sure that change is seen as a legitimate process.

I once had a friend say that I constantly try to bring humanity into the profession, and that's what I tried to do here. I am desperately worried we will lose our brightest teachers and leaders because they are overworked; so with that concern in mind, this book is as much for policymakers as it is for district and building leaders. We need to take time to de-implement what doesn't work in an effort to keep implementing what does work. Our profession is at stake.

Thank you for engaging in this work with me.

DISCUSSION QUESTIONS

1. What was the most difficult aspect to finding a focus for your team's de-implementation?

2. Did you learn anything new about the members of your instructional leadership team?

3. Was there any part of the cycle of de-implementation that you enjoyed more than others?

4. Is there a part of the cycle of de-implementation you did not enjoy? Why?

5. How will you use this process next?

One Final Activity

As I wrote in the book, the inquiry process should be fluid. As we go through it, we learn what works and what doesn't, and plan accordingly. When your team has time, I would like you to engage in a SWOT analysis of your de-implementation process.

SWOT stands for *strengths*, *weaknesses*, *opportunities*, and *threats*, and I would like your team to list your thoughts about the process using this analysis.

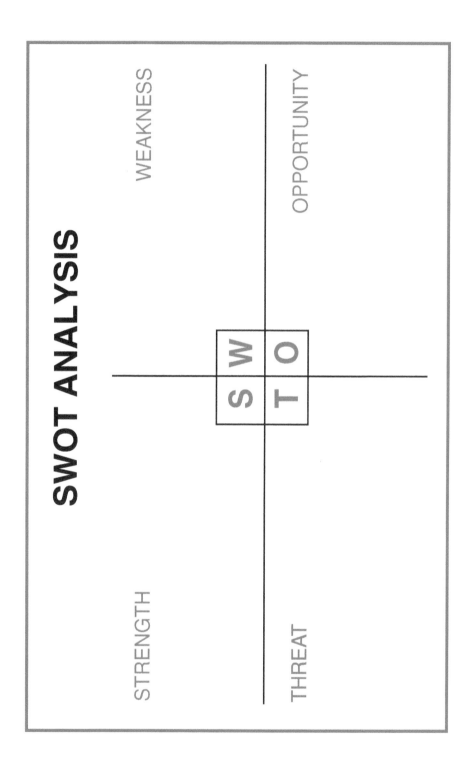

References

American Psychological Association Zero Tolerance Task Force. (2008, December). Are zero tolerance policies effective in the schools? An evidentiary review and recommendations. *American Psychologist, 63*(9), 852–862. https://doi.org/10.1037/0003-066X.63.9.852 . PMID: 19086747.

Anderson, L. W., & Krathwohl, D. R. (2001). *A taxonomy for learning, teaching, and assessing: A revision of Bloom's taxonomy of educational objectives* (1st ed., Abridged). Pearson.

Bandura, A. (1997). *Self-efficacy: The exercise of control.* Freeman.

Boston Consulting Group. (2014). *Teachers know best: Teachers' views on professional development.* Bill & Melinda Gates Foundation.

Brandt, M. J., & Sleegers, W. W. A. (2021). Evaluating belief system networks as a theory of political belief system dynamics. *Personality and Social Psychology Review, 25*(2), 159–185.

Butrymowicz, S., & Mader, J. (2017, November 11). Low academic expectations and poor support for special education students are 'hurting their future.' *Hechinger Report.* https://hechingerreport.org/low-academic-expectations-poor-support-special-education-students-hurting-future/

Casey, L. (2014). Questions, curiosity and the inquiry cycle. *E-Learning and Digital Media, 11*(5), 510–517.

Chen, W. W., Cato, B. M., & Rainford, N. (1999). Using a logic model to plan and evaluate a community intervention program: A case study. *International Quarterly of Community Health Education, 18*(4), 449–458. https://doi.org/10.2190/JDNM-MNPB-9P25-17CQ

Craig, H. L., Wilcox, G., Makarenko, E. M., & MacMaster, F. P. (2021). Continued educational neuromyth belief in pre- and in-service teachers: A call for de-implementation action for school psychologists. *Canadian Journal of School Psychology, 36*(2), 127–141. https://doi.org/10.1177/0829573520979605

DePaul University Teaching Commons. (2022). Direct versus indirect assessment of student learning. *Teaching Guides.* https://resources.depaul.edu/teaching-commons/teaching-guides/feedback-grading/Pages/direct-assessment.aspx

Dewey, J. (1911). Restricted outlook. *Journal of Education, 74*(1), 10–10. https://doi.org/10.1177/002205741107400108

DeWitt, P. (2021). *Collective leader efficacy: Strengthening instructional leadership teams.* Corwin/Learning Forward.

Donohoo, J. (2013). *Collaborative inquiry for educators: A facilitator's guide to school improvement.* Corwin.

Drucker. P. (2018). *2017 Drucker Prize reading module 2: Drucker on planned abandonment.* Drucker Institute. https://www.drucker

.institute/wp-content/uploads/2018/08/Reading_Drucker-on-Planned-Abandonment-1.pdf

Dutta, U. (2019, January). Addressing contextual challenges in underserved indigenous spaces of the Global South: In search of an approach based on unlearning, co-learning, and relearning. *International Journal of Qualitative Methods, 18.* doi:10.1177/1609406919891267

Esquivel, P. (2021, November 8). Faced with soaring Ds and Fs, schools are ditching the old way of grading. *Los Angeles Times.*

Farmer, R. L., Zaheer, I., Duhon, G. J., & Ghazal, S. (2021). Reducing low-value practices: A functional-contextual consideration to aid in de-implementation efforts. *Canadian Journal of School Psychology, 36*(2), 153–165.

Farvis, J., & Hay, S. (2020). Undermining teaching: How education consultants view the impact of high-stakes test preparation on teaching. *Policy Futures in Education, 18*(8), 1058–1074.

Feldstein, A. C., & Glasgow, R. E. (2008). A Practical, Robust Implementation and Sustainability Model (PRISM) for integrating research findings into practice. *Joint Commission Journal on Quality and Patient Safety, 34*(4), 228–243.

Fullan, M. (2007). *The new meaning of educational change.* Routledge.

Grant, A. (2016). *Originals: How non-conformists move the world.* Penguin.

Grant, A. (2021). *Think again: The power of knowing what you don't know.* Random House.

Gruenert, S. (2008, March/April). School culture, they're not the same thing. *Principal.* https://www.naesp.org/sites/default/files/resources/2/Principal/2008/M-Ap56.pdf

Guskey, T. (2021, November). The past and future of teacher efficacy. *Educational Leadership.* ASCD. https://www.ascd.org/el/articles/the-past-and-future-of-teacher-efficacy

Hargreaves, A., & O'Connor, M. T. (2018). Solidarity with solidity: The case for collaborative professionalism. *Phi Delta Kappan, 100*(1), 20–24.

Hattie, J. (2012). *Visible learning for teachers: Maximizing impact on learning.* Routledge.

Hattie, J., & Yates, G. (2014). *Visible learning and the science of how we learn.* Routledge.

Hill, H. (2021, May 25). Why evidence-backed programs might fall short in your school (and what to do about it). *Education Week.*

Killion, J. (2003). Eight smooth steps: Solid footwork makes evaluation of staff development programs a song. *Journal of the National Staff Development Council, 24*(4), 14–23.

Le Fevre, D., Timperley, H., Twyford, K., & Ell, F. (2019). *Leading powerful professional learning: Responding to complexity with adaptive expertise.* Corwin.

Leithwood, K., & Jantzi, D. (2008, October). Linking leadership to student learning: The contributions of leader efficacy. *Educational Administration Quarterly, 44*(4), 496–528.

Levin, S., Scott, C., Yang, M., Leung, M., & Bradley, K. (2020). *Supporting a strong, stable principal workforce: What matters and what can be done.* NASSP, LPI.

McKay, V. R., Morshed, A. B., Brownson, R. C., Proctor, E. K., & Prusaczyk, B. (2018, September). Letting go: Conceptualizing intervention de-implementation in public health and social service settings. *American Journal of Community Psychology, 62*(1–2), 189–202. https://doi.org/10.1002/ajcp.12258. Epub 2018 Jul 3. PMID: 29971792; PMCID: PMC6175194

Nilsen, P., Ingvarsson, S., Hasson, H., von Thiele Schwarz, U., & Augustsson, H. (2020, January). Theories, models, and frameworks for de-implementation of low-value care: A scoping review of the literature. *Implementation Research and Practice.*

Queen, J. A., & Schumacher, D. (2006). A survival guide for frazzled principals. *Principal Magazine.* NAESP.

Rhinesmith, S. H. (1992). Global mindsets for global managers. *Training and Development, 46,* 63–69.

Riley, P. (2018). *The Australian principal occupational health, safety and wellbeing survey 2017 data.* Institute for Positive Psychology and Education/Australian Catholic University. https://www.principalhealth.org/reports/2017_Report_AU_FINAL.pdf

Robinson, V. (2018). *Reduce change to increase improvement.* Corwin Impact Leadership Series. Corwin.

Robinson, V. M. J., & Timperley, H. S. (2007). The leadership of the improvement teaching and learning: Lessons from initiatives with positive outcomes for students. *Australian Journal of Education, 51*(3), 247–262.

Scanlan, D., & Savill-Smith, C. (2022). *Teacher wellbeing index 2021.* Education Support.

https://www.educationsupport.org.uk/media/qzna4gxb/twix-2021.pdf

Schwartz, S. (2020, December 16). Is this the end of 'three cueing'? *Education Week.* https://www.edweek.org/teaching-learning/is-this-the-end-of-three-cueing/2020/12

Senge, P. (1990). *The fifth discipline: The art and practice of the learning organization.* Random House.

Slavin, R. E. (2010, August 10). Co-operative learning: What makes group-work work. In *The nature of learning: Using research to inspire practice* (pp. 161–178). OECD.

van Bodegom-Vos, L., Davidoff, F., & Marang-van de Mheen, P. J. (2017, June). Implementation and de-implementation: Two sides of the same coin? *BMJ Quality Safety, 26*(6), 495–501.

Wang, V., Maciejewski, M. L., Helfrich, C. D., & Weiner, B. J. (2018, June). Working smarter not harder: Coupling implementation to de-implementation. *Healthcare, 6*(2), 104–107. https://doi.org/10.1016/j.hjdsi.2017.12.004. Epub 2017 Dec 24.

Index

A SAGE Publishing Company

CORWIN HAS ONE MISSION: to enhance education through intentional professional learning.

We build long-term relationships with our authors, educators, clients, and associations who partner with us to develop and continuously improve the best evidence-based practices that establish and support lifelong learning.

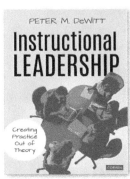

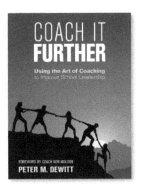